SUPERVISION AND COUNSELLING

by Gaie Houston

DEDICATED TO

Amely, Ann, Anne, Ari, Annette, Andrew, Adam, Alan,
Betty, Bernd, Barbara, Birt, Bridget, Bryan, Bill, Chris,
Christine, Christina, Claire, Clare, Calliope, Charles,
Christopher, David, Dina, Dermot, Dolores, Donna,
Diane, Diana, Del, Else, Eve, Elisabet, Elizabeth, Eric,
Flora, Frances, Guy, Greta, Giangiacomo, George,
Gavin, Gordon, Harold, Hans, Inge, Ita, Ishbel, Ivan,
Ian, Jane, James, Jackie, Jo, John, Joan, Joyce,
Johnnie, Judith, Jen, Jenny, Jeremy, Jan, Julian,
Jonathan, Julie, Joanna, Jerome, Keith, Karen, Kedzie,
Klaas, Kurt, Krissy, Lee, Lise, Liz, Lesley, Maggie,
Margaret, Mark, Mick, Mike, Mary, Marie, Marietta,
Marianne, Maurice, Mildred, Maja, Malcolm, Marthe,
Martha, Marty, Nelson, Nura, Naomi, Niko, Nancy,
Nina, Ole, Ofelia, Peggy, Pat, Petruska, Polly, Penny,
Rita, Richard, Roger, Stefan, Stephen, Sally, Sarah,
Toby, Tom, Troy, Ted, Tony, Tim, Tricia, Val, Vivian,
Wendy, Winston, Willy, Winifred, Windy, Yannis,
Xanthe.

THANK YOU!

CONTENTS

Foreword   page 1.

Critical Configurations   page 4.

Style and Method   page 8.

Rapport   page 17.

Keeping records   page 27.

Ethics   page 35.

Practics   page 43.

The Echo   page 53.

Getting Moving   page 62.

Staying Lively   page 70.

Skin Relation   page 78.

The Annual Review   page 85.

Other Fleas   page 94.

The Writer   page 100

FOREWORD

I asked a young therapist who comes to me for supervision what she expected from our sessions. "Well, supervision," she said, "You know, a sort of looking at the whole thing in perspective. I want really SUPER vision." She was not primarily asking that I should have this god-like overview. She wanted it for herself, as a product of what went on between us.

There is a good deal more to be said on the subject, and this book sets out to say some of it. But I liked her interpretation enough to put it here at the beginning. Put in another way, she had moved away from the notion of control, which is often associated with the word supervision. She was asking instead to be enabled. There are some tasks involving control for all of us when we supervise. We need to monitor people's fitness to practice. We need to make sure that practitioners work in conditions that encourage them to do the best job they can.

As well as setting boundaries and maintaining them, as I describe in part of this book, we have the fascinating work of using all our experience, to help develop our supervisees. They learn through their own pain, and mistakes, and triumphs. They can learn too through ours. At best we can work so that they finally go beyond us to become more than us. Supervising is immortality: it leads to the next generation of practitioners.

As the title says, this book is designed both for supervisors and their supervisees, be they called counsellors, therapists or psychotherapists. At different moments it evokes the peer, parent, poet, and many other facets of both parties to it. A good deal of what I write here echoes the manner of counselling supervision, and is addressed directly to the counsellor. Some of it is counsellor-training. To me that needs to be one component of useful supervision, along with many others. To that end, I have in the illustrative dialogues in some chapters, chosen topics which seem of themselves to contain teaching material. My hope is to present what is useful to people at many stages of their careers.

Supervision is literally an overview. So, simply taking the time and trouble to look again, in the presence of a supervisor, at what you and your patient have said and done, is a central task. Both of you search for a wider context, a fuller meaning. Is some quirk of the counsellor's responses the sign that she is beginning to play a role assigned to her by the client? Is she taking on that attitude he attempts to conjure from all around him?

In a supervision session, there is the opportunity to acknowledge emotions, suspicions, hunches, doubts, and much else that was partly or wholly suppressed at the time. With these out in the light, you are better informed, and so empowered to practice better.

Hearing what she says in what is likely to be the only discussion she has of her client, the counsellor improves her long view. She sees more clearly the strategy, the treatment plan that is forming in her own mind, alongside the agenda her client has talked of for himself.

Good supervision reminds the supervisee and supervisor to move in imagination from point to point of a benevolent human triangle, that of client, counsellor and supervisor. A counsellor who does nothing but attempt to see the world from the client's point of view, is denying her own responses to the client. If she concentrates on nothing but her own responses, she reduces the client's world to the counselling room, a microcosm of doubtful universality. If she dissociates constantly, looking only at the pair of them as a system, the client will be deprived of I-Thou experience. Several chapters of this book expand this central idea, and show practical ways to use it.

From the moment we began training, all of us were also, perhaps without acknowledgement, also learning to supervise. We were developing what Patrick Casement in his admirable book, On Learning from The Patient, called The Internal Supervisor. Now that supervision is formally required of more practitioners for the whole of their careers, there is the need to build on those silently acquired skills. As we learned to scrutinise, to search to understand, and sometimes forgive, sometimes celebrate, and sometimes change what we ourselves did, so now can those skills come out into the open to be used for other workers. What may need to be added are some drills that both save you trouble and improve your effectiveness. And, judging from the responses I had to a questionnaire to many supervisees, there is a need for vividness and variety, for sometimes using more than just words in your supervision time.

With the help of the considerable number of people I see as supervisor, and others, and with gratefulness for all that I have learned from them, I have put together these chapters. My hope is that they will help you to confidence, clarity, flexibility and rigour, and to pleasure in this aspect of your work.

A CRITICAL LIST OF CONFIGURATIONS

Before we go any further, let yourself think over the kind of supervision you want to give or receive, at your stage of your working life. A third-year student is likely to have different needs from a therapist of many years' practice. Someone seeing a few people in a voluntary setting may have different needs again from a full-time professional.

You need to feel secure, too, about the frequency of supervision. Every term-time week is what many students accustom themselves to. For that period between first and further qualification, 20 to 25 sessions a year are stipulated in many institutions in other European countries and in the States. In later life, if you work for an agency that allows you supervision, the budget may well affect the number of times you meet. The same may apply if you pay for yourself.

The British Association of Counselling requires its members to continue being supervised so long as they are working. As I write, some other professional bodies of various creative therapies are considering the same requirement. Maybe our anxieties about One Europe are bringing about an over-reaction. Be that as it may, the many years thus represented for many people, give scope for plenty of change and experiment.

I have a good deal of evidence that uninspired or wrong-headed supervision can be done in any setting. I have hard evidence too that excellent work can be done in many conventional and unconventional configurations, some of which are listed here.

Some good supervisors charge a lot of money. So do some awful ones, to my mind. The best supervision I have ever had was well on in life, in a peer group, for no money. So, if you are free to choose how you are supervised, consider your needs, and creative ways to meet them, rather than looking first at the constraints on you. To help your imagination, here is a reminder list of some configurations.

1.   *REGULAR ONE TO ONE SESSIONS with a designated supervisor, probably from your own discipline or training establishment. This is usually the first, and sometimes the only kind of supervision some people have. For anyone in training, this can be of enormous influence, and at best of inspiration too. "There needs to be supervisory holding by an experienced person who believes in the student's potential to be in tune with the patient and to comment helpfully." Patrick Casement.*

2.   *REGULAR ONE TO ONE SESSIONS with a supervisor from a different discipline. If this comes about because that supervisor is the only one you know of within fifty miles, there may be a sense of compromise in choosing her or him. If the choice is to do with extending your range, both of you need to acknowledge that, and find ways to include some training and discussion of your different philosophies in your hours together.*

3.   *ONE TO ONE PEER SUPERVISION, in which each of you alternate roles. You may alternate from week to week, so first one, then the other has a whole session focussing on her work with clients. Or you may alternate within the session, so both have a chance to deal with some of your preoccupations about how you are working. On postgraduate training courses I have introduced this way of working, alongside sessions with a staff supervisor too. In this way, people overtly learn to supervise as well as to counsel. In all these one to one arrangements, there is much to be said for letting the supervision session reflect the amount of time the supervisee would spend with a patient or client. This allows a training in pacing. Fifty minutes is thus a likely duration.*

4.   *GROUP SUPERVISION WITHIN YOUR DISCIPLINE. Some group supervision is mostly individual*

*supervision with a sympathetic audience. At the other end of the
spectrum, it can be a slightly frantic jostle, where everyone wants
their turn, and the supervisor may feel like a bird confronted with
five or ten gaping beaks in a crowded and noisy nest. Again, the
supervisor can be used to chair a valuable exchange between
informed people, the group members, rather than to represent the
Voice of Truth for the group.*

*5.   GROUP SUPERVISION IN A HYBRID GROUP. For
this you need a supervisor who is good at working with groups. At
best she will also be at home with most of the disciplines in the
room. If the group members are experienced, however, then
knowing all about Moreno and all about Melanie Klein may be less
important for the supervisor, than knowing how to enable people to
use the group to best effect.*

*6.   PEER GROUP SUPERVISION. Before you have much
experience, you are likely to have well-founded suspicions about
your own skills. So you need someone with more experience to help
you discover what on earth else you might do with this depressed or
that evasive client. A time comes when you have practised your own
discipline enough to feel reasonably confident within it. You may
know this is where you have got to, when you begin to feel
dissatisfied with the constraints of, say, endless two-chair work, or
forever offering careful interpretations. Further training is one
answer. Another is to meet people from other disciplines, to let them
look with their eyes at your work, and so to enrich your own ways of
responding by learning from your peers.*

*The length of a group supervision session needs to represent a
balance between the number of people in the group, the frequency of
meeting, and everyone's attention span. If the group is large, then it
will be more effective if members work in sub-groups or pairs for
part of the time.*

*7.   NETWORK SUPERVISION. This is a combination of
group and pairs. A number of people who want supervision meet as
a group at, say, monthly intervals. They may meet with an outside
supervisor, or as a peer group. The meeting will consist partly of
case presentation, or some other form of direct supervision. It is*

*also the forum for discussing some of what goes on at interim,
probably weekly, meetings, of pairs of group members. Partner
swapping can be arranged, and difficulties dealt with.*

*I invented this model, and shall not be surprised to find that many
other people have invented it as well, since it is so useful. The first
motive for me was to find a way to stay in touch with postgraduates
who worked odd hours, lived at a distance from each other, were
short of money, and still wanted to work with me.*

*Our monthly meetings, which lasted three hours, let me do some
overview work with them, and let them all meet each other. The
pairs between whiles gave scope for everyone to have more
individual attention, combined with flexible times and journeys, At
the same time, they were all in fact training themselves as
supervisors. And we spent some of our monthly meetings working at
how they could do that better.*

*8.   TRIAD SUPERVISION. This is an informed extension of
the common training device of working in threes, with one person as
counsellor, one as client and one observer. By halfway through
training, this observer role can well be extended, and re-named
supervisor. For perhaps the only time in the counsellor's career, all
three angles of the supervisory triangle are present at one time. The
temporary supervisor can practice challenging the counsellor to
account for what she did at different moments. The client will be
there to say what was really going on for her. From this book or
other sources the person in that role can equip herself to work
overtly at supervisory skills, at the same time as the other two work
at the skills of being client and counsellor.*

This list may serve to jolt you into thinking of yet a
different way of working. Good. Whatever the style, you need to be
sure that the person being supervised is

*Held, listened to, encouraged;
Challenged, confronted, stimulated
Disciplined, informed, answerable.*

If you manage all that fluently, read no further!

STYLE AND METHOD

There must be almost as many ways of working as a psychotherapist or counsellor as there are practitioners. Vive la difference. We are not clones yet, and even if we were, the weird and creative ways in which we translate our experience, probably means that many of our responses to each other are beyond genetic programming. That makes me happy too.

So, at best, the way you supervise will also be a unique mix of what you have learned, what you are skilled in by nature, and most formatively, your attitude. There is not one way to be a good supervisor. In your head you know that already. Please remember it again as you read what I say, or listen to other people's One Secret or Six Essentials of the subject. Some topics, I admit unwillingly, can be taught effectively in a climate of terror. I was once a dab hand at Latin Grammar, solely because of my fear and loathing of the scornful young woman who taught us.

To my mind supervision is best learned in the same mode as counselling is done. That is to say, as writer and reader, we shall do well to stay appropriately secure of what we do know and believe, open hearted in understanding, and excited at the possibility of making some changes. In other words, I hope we can both be more loving than fearful: that you can develop your own style of work, rather than search for the latest unhatched or new-fledged orthodoxy.

As you develop yourself as a supervisor - a lifetime's work, you need to keep an eye on how far your work resembles a counselling session. The next chapter sets out my strong arguments for keeping a good deal of the same attitude and style in the two kinds of work.

Even here there are some caveats. As far as I can see, every counselling method worth its salt will help a counsellor to do a decent job of enabling a client to look more deeply and or widely at her life, and set about change if she is so inclined. Too, every school of psychotherapy and counselling seems to me to suggest a focus, which probably has a great deal to do with the personality of its inventor. Since no human manages perfect and total vision, there are likely to be blind spots as well as areas of great illumination in every theory and resulting method.

Most interestingly to me, each method not only has its own restrictions of frame in the way it views behaviour; it seems likely to attract practitioners who tend to pick up or already have in their own personality some of the advantages and the disadvantages of the bias of the original theorist. Rather than now telling yourself that the system you have chosen to work by is completely the bee's knees and the cat's pyjamas, and takes care of all human, even all superhuman and transcendental behaviour and motivation, I counsel you to be humble. You may well be so, and will have puzzled already over what irrational let-offs you have allowed yourself in your particular method.

If you work in an interpretative way, perhaps you may wonder whether you are quite comfortable with contact and intimacy. If you work in a spiritual mode, how at ease are you, say, when clients want to deal with their carnality?

When you are supervising, it is just as important to look at what makes you do whatever you do; then you are in a stronger position to decide if you are doing what is most effective. It is part of your business to have overview, not just of the counsellor and client who make up the other two angles of the supervisory triangle, but too of the philosophy and method that are being used or assumed.

A different caveat about making supervision just like counselling, is that is all it may become. The supervisee may drift into using her time primarily for her own soul-healing. This is a very important task. It is one proper to her own therapy, though. If as supervisor you stay all the time in the didactic mode, the gain for the supervisee may be some free one-to-one training. The disadvantages may include her becoming dependent, relying more on you and thinking less for herself. A disadvantage for you is that, unless you are very fond of hearing yourself pontificate, you will get tired. A graver possibility is that the supervisee begins to run her counselling like your supervision, and devotes some of her time there to telling her client the meaning of life and how to live it.

The supervisor is an immensely influential person. You may have been more aware of that when you were a supervisee, than when you sit in the opposite chair.

In other chapters I write about using transcripts, sound and vision tapes, and other devices, learning aids which I see proper to supervision. Over-used, I see all of these as stopping the dialogue, the subtle dance between you and the supervisee. If you have the habit of looking every week at written transcripts she has prepared, think for a moment of the words, just the words, of the Hallelujah Chorus. Not much, huh? The music is most of that chorus. In the same, albeit subtler way, the melody of the counselling session, the music of what goes on in the supervision session itself, can, and needs to, inform and inspire both of you.

Some other interruptions of the I-Thou may show as clearly in pictures as words. To me they only look bad when they have reached caricature point, as here.

You do not have to turn yourself into a copy or update version of someone else to be a good supervisor. Here, as in counselling, we have the magnificent opportunity to stay in what I call a working dialogue. By this, here, I mean a conversation in which there are clear rules and assumptions. A central one is that your goal is to do whatever seems most likely to send the other person away more aware, informed, skilled and encouraged than she was when she came in. For once in life, there is an overt contract for you to enable another person. It is hard for me to think of any more exciting, any more gratifying, task.

As in counselling, you know that this overall goal is not likely to be met by your feeding toffees to your client. Short-term rewards may sometimes be bad for long-term health. There are going to be days for high-fibre, hard-to-chew offerings, even on occasion for doses of brimstone and treacle. Just as in counselling, again, you know that the peril in all this is that you become a little high on the power your authority gives you. The other person in the dialogue is the one who confesses her poor judgement and mistakes along with her successes. From the security of the outsider position, it is often easy to see what could or should be done. From there it is only the smallest shuffle to reach a place of secretly thinking that you would never have been as daft as the supervisee says she was. Not so.

The other end of this spectrum is to lapse into feelings of total inadequacy because you do not have a complete answer for a problem your supervisee brings you. As a counsellor I doubt that that would be one of your goals. You know in that setting that the client's own answers are more use than yours. You know too that you are doing her no good if you present yourself as an unattainably clever or wise demigod. But this form of insecurity rears its phantom from garbled memories of school, for many supervisors I have helped to train. You are not meant, as supervisor, to be a walking encyclopaedia or handbook of psychiatry. Reference books exist so that people do not have to carry vast amounts of specialised knowledge in their heads all the time.

There is a theory that groups will always be of one of four kinds. I think it applies well to supervision. One possibility is that task dominates, to the exclusion of feeling. That is what can happen if you and your supervisee spend all your time in then-and-there talk, diagnosing the absent client, or batting on about theoretical issues, say.

Another attitudinal set is that emotionality takes over completely. If something very horrible or wonderful has just occurred, that for a moment seems proper. But I have come across at least two emotion-led forms of supervision, which were simply not supervision at all except in name. In one, the supervisee is let to use the sessions for a kind of unending emotional scab-picking, neither therapy nor confessional, but a gossipy moan about her life, occasionally her clients, and all her hard times. When I challenged the supervisor in the pair I am thinking of, about her attitude to the supervisee, she said crossly, "Let her rot!" Hm. At least as destructive, and in the same mode, is the pair characterised by mutual resentment or contempt, who seem resolved to give each other as little as possible. What they do give are headaches and general ill-feeling.

The third kind of group or pair is one in which the emotionality shapes the task. A group manifestation is demo, perhaps, or a carnival. An evangelical spirit whooshes up some action. Most of the time, an evangelical spirit in the supervisor seems to me likely to deny whatever spirit there is in the other person in the partnership. Then I think of a project for counselling single parents, in which the workers' morale sank very low as they discovered just how bad the lives of the small children of these particular parents were. The grandmotherly presence of a particular evangelical supervisor was probably what saved the project.

In the last kind, the task shapes what happens, and the mood of the people is appropriate to the task. That I suppose is what we can usually aim for with most hope of being effective.

In supervision you may allow a little more befriending, and ordinary social exchange than with counselling clients. I assume that people who come to me for counselling are paying for a serious work-time, of a predictable, in some ways austere, format. On the other hand, if a supervisee I know well arrives at a time when I want a coffee, or when I suspect she has not had time to have a meal, we may very occasionally have a coffee together as we work.

There are counsellors, and indeed schools of counselling, which favour this amount of informality, even bonhomie, between counsellor and client. Many others do not. Make sure that your supervisees are clear in their minds on where they and you stand on these topics.

Other schools favour various forms of contract-making with the client. I see the advantage of letting the counsellor practice this contract-making from an opposite role, and negotiate with the supervisor about what they will agree between them. What are the bones, the central requirements you have of your supervisee, that you want to spell out to her, when you have heard her demands from her side?

One of them is likely to be about written or otherwise recorded and commented actual material from her sessions. I vary what I ask from people, according to their temperament, level of skills and experience, and in recognition of the demands of the rest of their life. In doing this, I am at pains to keep the developmental needs of the counsellor, rather than the contingency needs of some present difficulties, in the foreground.

PAT: When the baby's born I don't think I shall have time for any more verbatims for a while.
SUP: Tell me how long a while is.
PAT: A few months, anyway.
SUP: So you want to make time for counselling, but not for writing up fully.
PAT: We'll need the money for the mortgage.
SUP: Try sitting in the seat opposite you and being the first client who comes to see you after your baby is born. [PAT CHANGED SEATS, AND BURST OUT LAUGHING, THEN STOPPED UNEASILY.]

*PAT: I straightaway imagined the baby was crying in the next
room. And as myself...*
SUP: Come back to your own chair and say it.
*PAT: [DOES SO] I don't want you here, I want to pick the baby
up.*

As a result of this conversation, Pat decided to see clients
in a hired room for a while. Our supervision contract, which is what
she had begun to re-negotiate, then came back into focus. She was
to take a three-week break anyway at the time of the birth. After
that we settled on a six-week arrangement. In that first six weeks
she would aim to make brief notes of all sessions, and to bring me
some edited sound-tape of each of her few clients. When the six
weeks finished, she would decide with me on a plan for the next six
weeks.

It would have been easy for me to respond just to Pat's
side of the story. I wanted to make her aware of more of her own
needs than just the urgent one for money. And my need as
supervisor was to feel secure that I was not encouraging her to do a
third-rate job for her clients, nor the baby, nor herself. The review
time was an insurance around dignity. It gave us the chance to
make any new plan that was suitable, without it seeming like a
capitulation or failure.

Some of my intention in this chapter has been to remind
you that counsellors are very likely indeed to copy some of
supervision when they are counselling. As supervisor you need both
to be worth copying, and to keep an extremely lively eye on what is
appropriate to supervision sessions, and less useful for the
supervisee to take back as a method into her work.

Briefly, here are some of the useful likenesses I see
between counselling and supervision.

1. Giving time to hear what is said and what needs next to
be expressed - respecting the material.

2. Giving space to the client to find answers to difficulties.

Here are one or two of the differences in supervision.

1. On occasion you work faster, in a more focussed and critical style.

2. An overview is required from the supervisee, in a way that might be quite inappropriate in counselling.

3. There is likely to be more teaching and reference to theory.

4. In my view, the supervisor is free to be less careful than with some counselling clients. There is room for the wise tygers of wrath, and donkeys of daftness, as well as the horses of instruction. Recreation, in the best sense of the word, is available to all of us in supervision.

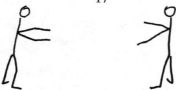

RAPPORT, AND BEING YOURSELF

This topic is not always taught explicitly, though the word is mentioned on most training courses. Rapport, or the lack of it, is the base on which all the work between you and your client is founded. In my view it is just as important in supervision. Whether or not you mean it, you are likely to transplant into your counselling the attitudes you pick up in supervision. Interest, respect, honesty, warmth are a few of the words that came up most often when I did a survey of supervisees' requirements of a good supervisor. So here is a chapter which I hope may have some new clarity on this starting-point subject.

As supervisor, you need to be open enough to yourself to know what you are teaching by example. I remember one of my supervisors, in many ways a very wise man, but reticent with his bad feelings. I can be better at that game than is good for me or honesty, so we sat there week after week inventing a world of reasonableness. He moved abroad, so I did not even challenge him about the tepid warmth between us, which had cooled to a setting point of boredom by the time he left. Then I went to someone who was a terrible intellectual showoff, and also talked into and over every sentence I started. She had so much to teach me that I put up with her style, while noticing how competitive and polysyllabic I became with her. We both smiled very brightly and nodded as we carved each other up verbally.

I learned something from these two, which I am reminded of time and again when I do live supervision of student psychotherapists. Dancing to the tune of the dominant member of a pair is a prevalent human response. A cheery counsellor may conjure false cheerfulness from a distressed client. A furious client may produce grovelling from the counsellor. The supervisor needs time and again to help the counsellor see herself as the patient probably does. Then they can work out whether the counsellor is pandering to the client, or fighting, or being in rapport. Rapport is perhaps easier to recognise than to measure. As I think about it, I guess tentatively, that some of the people I supervise, those whose work I specially admire, seem to function on two levels of it.

IMMEDIATE RAPPORT

This is phenomenological, a response of the moment. It exists partly as physical feelings. In me they seem like a slight excitement in the chest, a loss of fear of the person opposite, a confidence that we can, at least for part of our time together, be in tune with each other. The image that comes to me is of talking across a garden gate in good weather, rather than shouting greetings from our respective house windows. We are both within our boundaries, and yet we are close enough sometimes to touch each other. We are experiencing a form of synergy, an adjusting of my breathing and other body rhythms, even my brain waves, to complement, to be nearer the experience, of the other person. This rapport makes for an open learning and creative state. It has a lot to do with liking or not liking. Each person shows herself, rather than edits herself first. When I have heard what I have said, I may disagree with myself. The other person's statement may sound nearer the truth - or further off. When we disagree, neither of us has the sense of attacking the other person or being attacked. We are searching to express something the best way we can.

This level of rapport is spun in the moment, and is vulnerable to what the other person does. Her change of expression, or brusque movement, or the content of what she says, may influence me to be on guard, out of rapport. Out of rapport, I need to defend myself against her. I want to maintain who I am and what I believe. I may start to feel hostile, as fear mounts that she is in some magical way threatening all that I am. As I have said, it is a dysfunctional state to be in constantly in counselling or supervision.

THIRD EYE RAPPORT

I said I suspect that rapport works at two levels. Perhaps a better description is of a spectrum. At one end is the truth of the moment, in all its simplicity and complexity of smell, sight, sound, memory, anticipation, the impact or lack of it of one person on another. This lively, fragile, moment-to-moment rapport is the stuff of intimacy and life, as well as some of counselling. At the other is the ability to look at the person opposite in a large context, using a wide angle lens with great depth of field. The counsellor or supervisor, in some ways like a wise parent, needs to store up a data bank of rapport material. This has a lot to do with love, and with an awareness of more than the immediate present. For psychotherapists whose method is to suppress many of their own immediate responses, in the interests of the transference, this level of rapport is important to their own psychic health as well as their patient's. Let me explain myself.

Your six-year-old is rude to a visitor, or kicks your shins, or in some other way hurts or shocks you. Unless you are very insensitive or over-controlled, you are likely to roar at her or hit back. In my view, and I hope in yours, only a scared and foolish parent immediately concludes that she or he is dealing with a child who is innately an evil being who from now on for ever must be controlled rather than trusted. Winnicott's good-enough parent recognises that the young kicker or show-off of this moment is the same child who gave her sweets to her crying sister, who, unasked, carried food upstairs to you when you were ill, who showed love and generosity in a thousand ways many thousand times in her short life. You still trust and love the child, the moment you have finished the frowning or yelling of the instant.

Counsellors and psychotherapists have a whole range of possible responses to a symbolic shin-kicking from a patient. Whatever they say or withhold at that moment, they need also to be aware of whether they have enough interest and belief in the kicker, to be prepared to go on working honestly. When someone new to me in supervision begins to talk about a client as borderline, or possibly not ready for counselling, I wonder aloud about the counsellor's side of that comment. Yes, there are certainly people who can be described in these ways. But is this counsellor recognising something else which is valid and important to recognise, that her skills do not stretch to working with this client? Or is she saying that she simply feels frightened and vindictive? She has failed to recognise the stuff on which her underlying rapport databank could be built?

For example, however silent and apparently sulky a client is, she did actually get herself on the train and along the street and up the steps into your room. That is a statement of need or hope, of potential rapport, which is so obvious that in my experience counsellors often forget even to notice it. Again, every rejection, distraction, over-projection, misunderstanding, dismissive response, piece of blame, of placating insincerity, half-truth, whopping lie, can paradoxically be used as material for your store of underlying rapport. It is evidence of the client' extremely lively sense of other people, of you. It shows the amount of power, the amount of threat, she attributes to you.

We all want rapport, synergy, love, as a large part of our psychological, and so of our actual, survival strategy on this earth. If like me you believe this, then all the frustrating games a client plays are her personal failures, failures which by the time she gets to seek your professional skills, are probably deeply entrenched habits. So I hope to look with some love at all those aspects of a client which in supervision may also make me groan and grimace about her. She is repeatedly showing me, for example, how she keeps herself lonely or disliked. Looking with what in some belief systems is called the third eye, I may know the uselessness of re-enacting The Other, who usually walks out or shouts back or sneers or does whatever the client seems literally hell-bent on cajoling me to do. I feel in my bones, as you probably do, that if I start off a session feeling defensive, grim, narrow-eyed, I have probably reduced to zilch my chances of doing any useful work for the client. This is where third eye rapport is immensely important.

It is an easy thing to point out that rapport matters. Often, the harder task is to feel it, maintain it and communicate it. So what on earth is the counsellor or supervisor supposed to do? The great majority of people who come to me for counselling are, at least consciously, co-operative and open and invested in an obvious way in their own change or recovery. Unconsciously they may display a little of what I was describing in these last paragraphs. So, thinking of them, as well as the few people who are more overtly difficult to be with, here are a few of the ways I have seen succeed in making rapport. One is to keep yourself from being mesmerised. How often have you said, or heard people say that they felt drawn in to a client's game? That is what I call being mesmerised. When I question counsellors closely, I find that those who manage not to stay drawn in or sucked in or mesmerised, have a capacity for looking at their client in a large context. For example, when someone contradicts me, I can let myself tunnel down to a vision of the world which is no bigger than the verbal fight of the moment about who said what, when, and why. Victory is my aim. My good name or good sense are what I am fighting for. This is an invigorating pastime. It is not always an appropriate one when I am counselling.

Here is a disguised transcript of Claud being counsellor to Maggie, to illustrate what I am saying. The commentary has in it some of what we talked about when we looked at tape of the session in supervision.

M: *[Lies back in her chair and stretches arms above her head, keeping eye-contact with Claud] I don't know what to talk about today. [Smiles]*

C: *[Is aware of feeling sexually aroused. Finds he is grinning back. Now feels alarmed. Maggie is very attractive. Images of throwing himself upon her come to his mind. All this is happening in a nanosecond, but he feels an instant of panic, now imagining headlines in all the tabloid newspapers about him. No longer a psychotherapist, but Psycho The Rapist. All this florid imagining*

22

prompts him to draw back, to perceive Maggie and her statement in a larger context than just the intensity of Now. One context is his gestalt training about polarities. He could invite her to explore the polarity, to try out the statement that she does know what she wants to talk about. Her body-posture certainly gives some hints.
Another context he goes to, another part of the background, is that Maggie has told of men always chasing her, and her feeling so upset by this that she rejects them forcefully. If he confesses his sexual feeling, he may sound like these other men. What to do?] Maggie, I suggest you tune in to what you want ME to do about your not knowing what to talk about.

M: *[Easy and flirtatious, rather little girl]* O, I don't know. I just want you to do it! I don't want to be this responsible grown-up. I want to be naughty today.
C: Naughty. *[We both noted in supervision, as he did all too clearly at the time, that at this point Maggie put her feet about a foot apart, so that she was lying back in a way that looked very sexually receptive.]*
M: I do get tired of all this therapy. I'd like to know you in another way, outside these sessions.
C: I'm curious about how you see this other way of knowing me.
M: O, you know. Just talking and being friends and going for a meal or something. You're being a bit boring today.
C: I'm looking at how you are sitting, and noticing that you've crossed your legs as I say that. You know my way of working. I refused your invitation to your birthday party last month. I don't have social contact with anyone while we are working together. And this looks like one of the times when that rule is useful to me. I find myself very sexually aware with you today. You understand, there is nothing I am going to do with those feelings except report them, and see if they have anything to do with what is going on for you. *[Claud spells this out exhaustively, as he is so struck by the apparent sexual innuendo of most of what Maggie has said and done, and of the complete denial which seems to go with it.]*
MAGGIE: *[TEASES]* Boring!

CLAUD: I can tell you, I'm not bored. I'm working hard over here. And I've the impression that you're putting all your attention into a game, and not noticing what the game is about.

This extract is, among much else, about rapport and confluence. It would have been easy for Claud on one hand to go for confluence, the apparent rapport of joining in the flirtation. On the other, he might have felt flustered enough by his own arousal, to button himself into a prim put-down. But he was secure enough in himself, and loving enough to Maggie, to stay easy, to fight her as an equal. My belief is that unless that good feeling had communicated to Maggie, so that she felt trusting of Claud, she would not have let herself have or admit the insight about loneliness.

The foundation of rapport is to learn yourself enough that you know what style you have, and when you are being truthful to yourself. This is much of what training should be about, and it is as well a maintenance task for supervision. You are always changing. In supervision you can comment and even practice some of those changes, with a helpful witness.

When I hear counsellors protest "But I couldn't do that! It's just not me!" I listen for whether there is panic or self-knowledge in their tone. Are you you when you are talking to the deaf old lady down the road? Doing the conga? Arguing at the supermarket check-out? Picking your nose? Playing ludo with your child? Of course you are. You are whatever you do. If you are at ease with yourself you will accept this. If you are more fearful, you probably hold on to an image of yourself, to which you try consciously to fit your behaviour, hacking away to make yourself fit this Procrustean bed.

A fact of life is that I and you are always part of a system. The conga is a system, a formalised romp. The supermarket check-out is a system with a role in it for you, that you can play in many ways. You probably need to take far more heed than many counselling courses encourage, in looking at the counselling pair, at you and the client, as a system. Unless you are very rigid in your personality, in which case you are not very likely to be working in this area, you will be at least subtly different with every person you work with. For a start, you are both talking about, and becoming part of, their life, which is different from every other life in the universe. Much more, you are responding to the countless signals that pass within or without words between you, and in so doing you are spinning a mass of invisible filaments between you, either of bridging, open lines, or of defense. Doing this is probably the most important part of counselling, most of the time. Making a mess of it is, like smoking, dangerous to your health and your client's.

Here is part of the second session of work with Esther, single, twenty-five, a beauty consultant who feels she has no friends, and a counsellor I think made a good job of achieving rapport. The account, like all I use in this book, is based on real happenings, and has had details changed to preserve the anonymity of the people in it.

E: [Smiles a great deal.] I feel so much better after our session. I really think you're great! I'm recommending a friend to you, do you mind?

C: [Smiles] You seem to have taken to me very quickly. I don't know what I did that makes you think I'm great. [Will Esther be direct, and so move towards intimacy, or avoid?]

E: O, you were really great. [Her voice is rapid and vague} And you've got lovely skin.

C: O, I like hearing that. And then I think, here am I looking at you from the point of view of my profession, counselling, and you're looking back at me from the point of view of your profession.

E: [Interrupts] I hope you don't mind me asking. Do you have highlights, or is it just the sun?

C: [For a second she retreats into defensive feelings, hating the thought that her hair might look dyed. Then her vision goes wide enough to take in the system of her and Esther. She laughs.] I don't think I'm doing a good job of work for you if I go off into talking about my hairstyle. [Is serious again] I'm aware that you came here saying you feel very isolated. So I'm making the guess that it's easiest for you to get on with people if they are beauty clients. I could easily start to feel like one here.

*E: [Looks sad, loses her beautician's smile] Except for phoning my
Mum at weekends, and we don't get on, I suppose that's the only
people I ever have a talk with, my clients.*
C: And now you're the client.
*E: It's hard to get hold of the idea that I don't have to do things
for you. [She looks at C, meeting her eyes for a second.]*
*C: I felt at ease, somehow in contact with you, as you looked at me
then. As if you had looked at me for you.*

I see that as a very admirable piece of rapport-building and
counselling, all in one. What the counsellor did was keep a wide
perspective, a large gestalt, however Esther narrowed hers down. I
think it would have been very easy to feel cornered, and give an
answer that sounded reproving, specially to the highlights question.
Direct questions about the counsellor's life are hard to deal with.
Factual answers can turn the session into a messy half-social chat.
Refusal to answer may puzzle and offend a client who is not at all
used to the game rules of counselling, which are markedly different
from those of ordinary social conversation. The counsellor here
stayed aware of what she knew about Esther's profession, and at
the same time her own boundaries. She did refuse to talk about
herself in a general way, but she did it from an attitude of good
feeling, rather than defensiveness. Then within a moment or two
she was more self-disclosing, in saying that she felt in contact with
Esther when their eyes met. It was part of this counsellor's style to
be very open about her responses to the client as they occurred.
Do you see that this is a very different form of self-disclosure from
telling about your child's measles, or the troubles you had getting
the lawn-mower serviced? Telling the client your here-and-now
responses may educate her about her effect on people. Telling her
about your visit to Buckingham Palace begins to make you into an
image, rather than a function, for her.

I feel different and show differently with, say, the woman
whose husband was killed when they were on their tenth
anniversary holiday; with the young man who told me he was
thinking of knifing his flatmate; with the girl who has just finished
her third bout of chemotherapy, and comes to see me in a

magnificent turban which covers her baldness. Each dance is a different one. In supervision too, I and you need to find the ways of being ourselves which communicates with the person supervised, and is effective in helping them with the craft skills of their counselling. Sense of competence is one reward. Another is finding a way of being aspects of yourself you enjoy and which seem appropriate, in each system.

KEEPING RECORDS

Enough people who come to me for supervision have had problems with writing up sessions, to make me address most of this chapter directly to them. I hope that as supervisor you let yourself read the chapter too, partly to notice where you have different and better ideas which you are reminded of in reading mine.

If you see very few clients, and are comparatively fresh to counselling, I do believe that you may carry full and clear memories of what they and you are doing in your sessions, without any writing up. However, that memory will not last too long in its springlike freshness. It is highly unlikely to last even with that client, if you go on seeing her for some months. It will certainly not last with clarity when you have moved on to other people.

A discipline for this bottom-line task is to imagine that you might be called into court to give evidence of your patient's whereabouts and state of mind on any of those dates when she was seeing you. You might be.

Now let yourself imagine two more scenes. One is of your client having some kind of breakdown, and asking you to talk with her doctor or psychiatrist. The last is of your client making a good ending of counselling with you, and saying in the last session, "By the way, I know you keep notes on me. I should rather like to have a look at them, or keep them." The answer to this last might even be no. What I am suggesting is that you keep your notes in such a way that you can give an unflummoxed answer to whatever questions are asked concerning them.

If you are as resistant as I can be to writing up notes properly, you will do well to make the task as inviting as possible, first by having ready appropriate writing materials. A large exercise book for each client may help you feel in charge. Or you may like to take a new sheet of loose-leaf paper for each session. Different-coloured folders for different clients can give a sense of good cheer. Next, you may do well to have a drill for writing up, which keeps you from rambling, and helps you include what is going to be most useful when you look back at your notes. Here are some ways for you to copy or adapt if you have not already settled on a method which suits you.

FACTS LEFT You can use the left hand page for facts: when your client saw you, whether she was late or early, whether her payments are up to date, what you did about it, what you talked about or did, and how you ended. The right hand page is for your feelings, hunches, opinions and reminders to yourself, as of any theme you want to focus on next time. At the bottom of the page you may want to note whatever you want to talk over with your supervisor.

MARGIN PAGE A very simple way is just to use the right hand page as an extended margin. On the left you write down everything you want to record. Then you read back, and as extra memories, or comments and ideas, come up in your mind, you put them opposite the relevant parts of the notes on the left.

ME RIGHT If you suspect that you can get too identified with your clients, you may like to keep the left hand page for the client's words and actions. and the right hand one for your responses. For clarity, it can help to offset what you write. So, if you start on the left with five lines quoting from or telling about your client, then you start writing at line six on the right, to describe your response. And so on.

BRACKETS The data of the session and the commentary may be interwoven, perhaps with brackets round the commentary, to indicate that you know when you are recording data and when you are surmising.

COLOURS Using a different coloured pen for overwriting different kinds of comment is another simple device which makes clear what you were doing, even when you return to the notes months later.

As a student you need to keep fuller and probably more laborious notes than you will later in your career. In training you are likely to write verbatim recalls of sessions, for example. Perhaps you do not, but just make sound or video records, from which you write extracts with commentaries. Both these useful devices are very time-consuming. From time to time, though, they are an important part of supervision in later life, giving you and your supervisor a chance to see if you play as good a game as you talk: reporting aloud often blurs some of the clumsinesses, the odd sloppy habit you acquire in the privacy of your one-to-one session.

Use your supervisor for talking over whether your present way of keeping notes deals best with the needs of all three of you in the supervision triangle. Your needs as the worker are at least as important in this area as those of the other two.

DATA AND COMMENTARY

Commentary should follow on the recording of good information., or data.

Good information is some of what you both actually said. Good information is your note of when you were pleased with what you said, and when you were uncertain or disapproving. Good information is a note about your emotional responses to your client. Taking the trouble to note down this data, you are, I hope, very likely to begin or continue to intuit, guess, opinionate inside yourself, about what else was going on in you and your client.

In many counselling courses, I have been dismayed to find that no distinction is made between what I am calling data and commentary. Even where that has been made clear, I have not seen much acknowledgement that there is a huge distinction to be made between your, the counsellor's, surmises about what may be going on in another person's life and mind, and about your own responses, unstated thoughts and feelings, and too your ideas of how to go forward when you next meet.

As you think of what I am saying here, you may come on other categories of what you can usefully include in your notes. One is the relation to theory. For the good of your practice, there is much to be said for making space in your notes, at least from time to time, for reminders of what was behind what you said. Put in other words, this means the theoretical justification for what you uttered. At a simple level, you may come to realise that you have fallen into some habit like asking far too many questions. Or you may have taken to being what you liked to think was empathic, but sounds on reflection more like collusive.

Well, how on earth are you going to let some or all of this information into the notes you make, probably at some speed each week, in the midst of an already busy life? You may have ideas that suit you. If not, here are some more suggestions that I know have worked for many of my supervisees.

MINIMUM EFFORT FOR MAXIMUM USEFULNESS.

If you ask people to tell their history at some length when they first come to you, this circumstantial information about them will inevitably be at the beginning of your notes, easily accessible when you falter in your memory of how many siblings they have, or whether their father died or ran off when they were two. Many counsellors, specially if they work for short times with people, do not begin like this. To them I recommend keeping space at the beginning of the file or notebook, in which to record the client's family history, stated reason for coming to counselling, and the counsellor's view of the most useful focus. Room needs to be left for adding new material as the sessions go by.

The headings in this section could be

1.   *NAME [probably coded] AND MEANS OF REFERRAL*
2.   *PRESENT CIRCUMSTANCES [Mrs A is 28, living since
she was eighteen with Claud. Works at Boots.]*
3.   *HISTORY [Leave plenty of room to put in facts about her
life and her ways of dealing with its events. You can add as the
weeks go by. Noting the date can be informative here.]*
4.   *REASON FOR SEEING ME [Has changed jobs three
times in the last few months, and thinks she is unreasonably difficult
with everyone at work, though she gets on perfectly, her word, with
family and Claud]*
5.   *MY HUNCHES [She said strongly out of the blue that she
was not thinking of leaving work and having a baby. I guess she is.
Longer-term work probably needs to be about her daring to
acknowledge her own needs, and admit the humanness of close
family, and therefore self.]*
6.   *TIMES AND PAYMENTS [Tuesdays at 11am, with 3-
week break at Easter when she will be abroad. One month paid in
advance, next payment due...]*

LETTERS

Many practitioners have a drill, of always sending new
clients a letter which sets out what you have in your first meetings
agreed between you, in terms of appointments, fees, notice of
ending, and anything else relevant to making a clearly defined
container in which the counselling can happen. In countries where
litigation is a popular hobby, this letter needs to contain some
disclaiming statements which have been read by a lawyer to see
that they make sense and have legal force. I do not know of many
people in the United Kingdom who yet do this last. Unfortunately
the possibility needs to be there in your mind. A copy of this letter
has its place at the back or front of your notes about that client,
along with copies of any other letters that pass between you. There

is sometimes great therapeutic value in being able to show a client that he or she is inventing history, by showing the discrepancy between what she says you agreed or wrote, and what is really there. The chapter on Practics has more about letters.

Find a set place for your notes, where you always keep them unless you are using them. At best this is a locked file drawer. If you keep your records on an open shelf, then I advise that you use no more than an initial to denote your client, and you keep his or her full details elsewhere. I can tell several hair-raising anecdotes to justify this advice. One is of a jobbing builder reading the counselling notes about his sister-in-law's marital problems. These were apparently lying in a named folder on a window-sill. Another is of a disturbed client's deliberately stealing the notes, again in a named folder, about her friend [and enemy] who came to the same counsellor. Another is of police coming to the flat where a counsellor had a room, with a search warrant which had nothing to do with the counsellor. But her files were taken away. Do all of these stories sound as if they could not possibly happen to you? I'm glad if it's true. What might go wrong in your case, then? Think about it and take precautions. In good counselling, clients show the substance of themselves, their fears and secrets and pain and irrationality and hope. They give you the power, very often, to destroy their good name. Shakespeare had pertinent things to say about that.

Making a habit of keeping notes is an aid to good practice, good learning, and peace of mind. Designate a time when you do your writing up, within 24 hours of the session. Straight afterwards is an excellent time, if you can manage it. Late at night suits others. Just be clear about your own method, and stay with it. Counselling needs to be a rigourous profession, even if you do it for no money, for few sessions a week. Nowhere is that rigour more needed than in steadily holding to a discipline of note-keeping.

Imagine giving answers that please you to an enquiry about your habits, your drill for taking, adding to, referring to and safely filing and storing your notes. Then make the story come true!

33

How much are you going to write? Consult yourself. You know if you are inclined to be laborious, and sit over writing jobs, hating them and elongating them, all at the same time. Do you need to? Talk to your supervisor about it. Or are you clever and quick and scatter-brained, and get by because, at least as far as you can remember, you have an excellent memory?

Whatever your personality, you need to find a way of writing up that suits you, that lets you monitor yourself, and that does justice to the work your client is doing in the sessions.

As a counsellor, I rarely look forward with any pleasure to writing up. Then when I begin, I am often fascinated. As a supervisor of practicing therapists, I will not accept anyone as supervisee unless she or he is willing to write notes, and occasionally write up a verbatim report of part of a session, for us to talk over together. In making that requirement, I am thinking of the people who are counselled. They deserve our trouble.

SUPERVISOR'S NOTES

I know supervisors who do not keep any notes. I know others who keep fairly complete accounts of their supervisees' sessions. I am averse to keeping records of what is third hand, that is to say, the supervisee's client's life-story. The notes that the supervisee brings along with her will tell me, or should tell me, as much as I need to know about all that.

What I need to keep in focus, and in my note file, is what I am observing about the supervisee herself. This may sound dreadfully obvious to you. But I have been astonished on many occasions to find supervisors simply and solely joining in with the counsellor as a backstop problem solver of the client's problems.

My supervision notes are much briefer than therapy notes. They contain details of dates, times, payment, for everyone. Then for newer supervisees I write more about their mood and manner, way of working, and possible gaps in their skills. With people I have known much longer, I jot down their theme, and a brief record of who they were talking about. Supervision notes will also contain the record of review sessions, or of my requests for verbatim recording or whatever. The notes show me whether a supervisee wants to spend many sessions talking on and on about one client, or tries to skitter like a pond-skater over problem points with six clients, every session.

By generally giving one page to each session, I can make the exercise book I use for each supervisee into a bring-forward file, reminding myself under future dates to ask particular questions, or comment on how they are getting on in some difficult piece of work, or new piece of training.

My notes are a surer check than my memory, that over a period we are acknowledging all the people the supervisee sees, and are keeping a balance in how we do that.

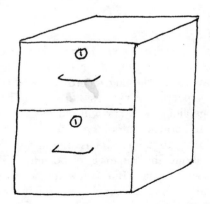

ETHICS

Whether she has noticed it or not, the counsellor or therapist has her own professional ethics. With the supervisor's help, she needs once in a while to talk these out. She is likely to be impressed and encouraged to work better when she reminds herself of her social goals, which is what ethics are about. The supervisor needs to know and agree with these ethics. Like all beliefs and rules, these are best left open to the possibility of change. There are a number of ethical questions for the supervisor herself to answer, too. This chapter is directed for the most part to them, and to the supervisor's place in the supervisory triangle.

Bridget Procter starts with the important simple vastness, What do you think people are for? You need your own answer to that, and you need it to be in line with what you are doing in your work. That does not have to mean that you have the same large beliefs as each supervisee. For me it would be unethical to pretend that I have their religious beliefs, or the same views of good and evil, when I do not.

Beside the ethics which make the largest context of your work, I feel clear about insisting on the right answers to many, apparently small, particular questions from the counsellor. I can start with something so obvious that it can be overlooked. Is she working in suitable conditions? Counsellors and therapists seldom have a Union to protect them, so the supervisor needs to be sure, for example, that the supervisee is not working alone in a building, particularly at night. I am thinking of one drop-in counselling service that was set up just near a psychiatric hospital in a large city. Until I objected, its counsellors took turns at having an evening alone in their open-doored Centre.

Further, the counsellors in this new service all had perfectly respectable counselling qualifications; none of them had experience of working with drop-out psychiatric patients dropping in upon them. My hair stands on end when I think of the possibilities.

A doorkeeper, a change to a by-appointment service, and their introduction to the nearby hospital, its staff and patients, were recommendations they accepted. If not, I would not have stayed as their supervisor. To my mind it is not ethical for the supervisor to gloss over the implications of such physical conditions, or of others, some of which are talked of in this chapter.

A rule of thumb is never to assume that your supervisee is being sensible in every respect. Check out. And stay with your beliefs.

My dress befits a Prince among Practitioners

Do not go on supervising someone whose practices makes you uneasy. You choose whom to supervise. If that is not the case, change it. If you thoroughly dislike someone, there is perhaps little incentive for either of you to work together, in counselling or supervision. If the other person seems mad, you may come to the same answer.

If you work in a training institution, supervisees may apparently be thrown at you in an arbitrary way. It is worse than useless to deal with patients or clients just because they are Sent. Both parties to supervision, too, need to want to work together. I can argue this with you. If you quote the student who is so difficult that no other staff are prepared to take her on, then to me the large question is whether she should go on being a student at all. What is more, the open choice offered to her, to put some goodwill and effort into the supervision, or leave, can be a salutary confrontation.

When I am accepting someone new as a supervisee, after they are in practice, I am looking at them in terms of their personality, and training, and willingness to learn. By their deeds shall ye know them. I only want to supervise people I would be prepared to recommend to clients. Moreover, just as people chatter about their therapist, so supervisees talk together about who they Go To For Supervision. Having them on my list or your list sounds like some kind of seal of approval of the way they work. Make sure you want to give it.

In counselling, I find it in myself to work with some people who are a pain in the neck, and I do it by functioning in part on what I have called third-eye rapport. In supervision, I am there to be an effective supervisor, and to enjoy myself. There is more room for me in the group or partnership, at least in the way I supervise. I put this near the beginning of a chapter on ethics, because I see this decision as an ethical one. I doubt if I could maintain reserves of patience for some difficult counselling clients, if I was constantly having to do the same with supervisees.

I do not want to tell you to do what I do, but to notice that there is a choice there to make, and to be clear how you are making it and whether you respect what you decide.

Irreverently, I spoke of some clients being a pain in the neck. That brings me to another choice. How fastidious are you going to be about maintaining proper respect for clients when you talk about them in supervision? Now, I do not see catharsis as the prime aim of a supervision session. But at times I condone or even encourage counsellors to complain, whine, shout or in some way blow off some of the frustration they find they have accumulated with one or another client. I see this as a quick route to lowering stress, giving perspective, and often, bringing humour to an otherwise gloomy memory.

Likewise, I blurt, I say my scepticism, I devil's-advocate, I make faces at times. I trust that my concern for the client as well as the counsellor is still understood. And I think I am both energised and energising. From time to time I spell out that some of what I am doing in the supervision session is private to that place, and not a suggestion to copy. You may prefer that whatever you say in supervision could be quoted to the counsellor's client without offending her. That cautious position seems to me an admirable one, provided it suits your personality.

That brings us to another decision, about confidentiality of supervision. One aspect of that is whether the supervisee is going to tell her client things you say. I know that at times I have been used as the stalking horse for uncomfortable confrontations. "My supervisor asked me if I thought you listened to anything I say." From a novice, this seems better than not tackling the subject. Most of the time, I would at such a moment want to see if the supervisee was setting up a splitting game, putting the bad feelings out of the room, on to the invisible third. If so, she is only secondarily being unethical. The worse is that she is colluding with or initiating wimpiness and muddle.

So far I have never had any difficulty about keeping quiet over what is told to me about clients · by the counsellor. As supervisor I, and you, are in a position of great responsibility to the client, and possibly too, of some prejudice. By that I mean, that we have only the counsellor's view of the client. There is no guarantee that that view is all the truth or nothing but the truth. With us, the client is in the perilous position of being on hearsay evidence. I need often to remind the counsellor and myself of that.

Now, the counsellor may or may not tell her clients that she will talk about them to me. If she does, I want her to be able to give an unequivocal assurance that whatever is reported to me will go no further. The person being counselled may not be over-comfortable at the idea of a stranger hearing at second-hand what he has been saying and doing with the counsellor. Then again, as many clients reportedly say, there is, beside this worry about exposure, a balancing feeling of safety, that the counsellor takes him seriously enough to talk about her work with him, with another professional.

If there are strains on confidentiality, as there can be, they are properly between the counsellor and the client. The supervisor is a third party. Take the example of a client who seems to be becoming mentally ill, loses insight, and says she will not see her doctor because all doctors are known to administer poison. That is a challenge to the counsellor. I am ready to give my opinion and advice about what the counsellor is to do, if she wants me to. But I myself am not the one put on the spot to do something or bite my nails: she is.

In the chapter on record-keeping I give advice about keeping notes safe. In doing so I assume that you are invested in keeping the privacy of whoever is working with you. In supervision, I still give great importance to keeping the privacy of that same client as intact as possible. I ask the counsellor only to refer to her clients by their first name. As well, I will not supervise counsellors about clients who are known to me. Again, this works most of the time, but not quite invariably.

Trainees in supervision often counsel their peers, for example. We do then impose a strict not-outside-these-four-walls rule of privacy. Again, I sometimes do live observation of therapists working with a group. Afterwards they talk about the members of the group in their general supervision. I enjoy the luxury of for once being able to put a face to a name.

I have worked with a supervisor who required me to use only an initial or cipher name for any client. I lapsed so often, and used so much energy reducing Ailsa to A or Peter to P, that I prefer the device I have talked of here. You may feel better with my supervisor's method, or with the omission of any name, and a convention of talking only of This Client. The underlying ethic is the same. If you think what I am saying is over-purist, please ponder again. Within training establishments, for example, staff are sometimes both therapist and supervisor, in other words evaluator, of the same person. I find it difficult to believe that this does not taint the content of the work.

Not infrequently, people new to being counsellors have very hopeful views about the personal responsibility of everyone. But circumstances alter cases. If I have a fit or a stroke or get run over, I am at that moment less interested in the moral question of whether I am totally responsible for getting myself into the disaster, than in surviving. I hope very much that other people will take on temporary responsibility for looking after me. I want to be held down or picked up or pulled out of the road, and I cannot manage that myself. It is sometimes less obvious when someone is mentally ill in a way that exposes them and others to possibly extreme harm. So I have an ethical requirement that anyone working as a counsellor under my supervision has at least a barefoot psychiatrist level of knowledge about signs of mental illness. And I want them to be in the sort of contractual arrangement with their clients, to let them act on their suspicions, without breaking promises. I am talking here of what in many counselling settings is going to be a rare occurrence indeed. But it is one to be prepared for.

Much more often, counsellors are likely to come across prospective clients who are on prescribed, or even illegal, drugs, or alcohol. There are ethical or pragmatic decisions to make here too. Again, they must be influenced by a counsellor's experience, or lack of it. As supervisor, you need to know enough to be able to discuss these difficult decisions in a way that is useful to your supervisee. Is she justified, for example, in saying that she will not work with anyone who arrives drunk or full of drugs? Is she right to say that she will not work with anyone who is abusing themselves with drugs or alcohol at all? Is it useful for her to counsel people on tranquillizers or mood-changing drugs? Is she going to insist on being in touch with their doctor if she takes them on? Does she look at these questions as ethical or pragmatic? How much are they either?

THE RESOURCE BOX

As a corollary to important and lively discussions on these topics in supervision groups, I ask for the establishment of a Resource Box. This is a file or box in which supervisees put copies of relevant articles on these specialist subjects. As well, they amass there a list of publications, agencies and people who might be of help, including sympathetic local doctors and psychiatrists, mental hospitals, social services, day centres, helplines, counselling and psychotherapy centres with whom they are in rapport , and much more. They keep a drug list, either M.I.M.M.S., or a simple one prepared by the local psychiatric hospital. This is an age of information.

Counsellors need an effective way of keeping up with what is happening and being thought in their area, their profession, their culture. I suggest that individual supervisees put together the same kind of file for themselves, and use the opportunity of training days or other meetings with peers, to exchange useful data. They could do worse than share out the reading of one of the few other books on the topic, "Supervision in the Helping Professions" by Robin Shohet and Peter Smith. Telling each other about the chapters is a social way of fitting useful reading into busy lives.

Doing such things is to me the demonstration of an ethical position, and a temperamental one. The counsellors are showing themselves still open to learning. One of the tasks of the supervisor is to encourage and maintain openness to learning from the outside world, and from the counsellor's own experience. The client will not get a proper service from anyone who has rigidified into an unquestioning orthodoxy in her work, or become a little vain about the correctness of her intuitions, or her general way of working. So, as supervisors, we need to work at staying as open and as sharp as we hope our supervisees will be.

Many ethical questions are dealt with under the simple headings

1. *What am I doing?*
2. *What for?*
3. *How?*

If the answers to those three mesh together, and mesh with the personality and training of the person answering, you or your supervisee are probably doing fine. They display the tactics of the work, the strategy or treatment plan, and the process of the work. There is an ethical as well as a practical need for the supervisor to be informed of all these, and to keep them in the supervisee's focus.

Now that accreditation of counselling and psychotherapy has become a hot topic, I find that some supervisees are in an ethical dilemma. Are they to pay good money to be an Associate of this or Affiliate of that organisation, in order to make themselves look respectable? They know themselves to be respectable already. They may greatly mistrust the skills or beliefs of other members of these same organisations. Are they, on the other hand, to stay independent, and perhaps end up outlawed?

There is a good deal to be said in many cases for joining an organisation which is large in relation to your profession. It is likely to be monitored by being in the public eye. What is more, if there are fights to be fought within it about standards or other subjects of great importance, any effort the members put in will benefit a good number of people.

This is for many people a new choice, to which the supervisor should not, I think, have an answer for them. She needs to offer her attention, even her arguments, as they come to their own conclusions.

PRACTICS

As the last chapter was about ethics, this one will do well to talk about some of the practicalities of supervision. The two are closely entwined. What I do is what I am. How I supervise constitutes an ideological statement, whether I want it to or not.

To make the point, I begin with an apparently tiny, and often overlooked decision. What is the counsellor going to do if she meets her client by chance outside the sessions? Working out at a first or early session, with the client, whether both parties are to ignore each other, or give a scanty greeting, or what, will help them both. In the same cause, I have found it necessary to remind supervisees never to leave explicit telephone or other verbal messages for their clients with third parties. Discreet professionals occasionally seem to have the most outlandish brainstorms. I like to guard against a few of them before they occur.

How you begin and end sessions is one of the many ways that what you do as supervisor may well be copied by your supervisee, when she is being counsellor. Notice what you are doing, and talk over with your supervisee any change you decide to make. I favour exact time-keeping, and open talk of any deviation from that.

As I would when counselling, I like to deal with paying and any arrangements about the time of our next appointment, at the beginning of the session. That makes it easier to keep to time at the end.

I have on occasion supervised people who have made appointments with their clients at one and a half hour intervals, to allow for the long-windedness of some of the people coming to see them. For both parties, I see this as a bad idea. With one such supervisee, I suggested that if she worked in this way, she might fix an hourly rate, and charge her client for each quarter of an hour or part thereof that she used. Doing this let some financial advantage back to the counsellor, and made it clear to the client that he or she was not a special case, who could have an hour and a half for the price of one hour.

In fact this supervisee moved to more conventional timings, after she had taken on board the way in which, without noticing it, she was setting up tensions with other colleagues. She discovered that local clients were beginning to say that if Mary let them have a nice long time, then why couldn't the other trainee therapists be as accommodating? In other words, Mary had without noticing drifted into what she came to see as unfair competition with her peers.

It is easy to be aware of the limited system, the small context, of you-and-the-supervisee, or you-and-the-client. We are also operating in the context of our relation to colleagues, to institutions and work places and family. Indulging the Ancient Mariner in your client has effects not just on you, but through all those systems too.

Many clients, and even some counsellors have an uneasy way of using time. Perhaps they procrastinate, and leave their most important statement till five minutes before the end. Perhaps they arrive late. Perhaps they arrive early, and seem determined to stay for the day if they can contrive it. Unless I keep with fair strictness to my times when I am working, I am going to get frazzled, and encroach on the time of the next client. Time and again, I have a shrewd guess that I would also, in going along with the other person's hazy time boundaries, be ineffective. If they use time as a weapon. I see it as my job to help them see if they want to change that. Just being disabled by that weapon, waiting for them to find their cheque book and diary, or tell me a last episode of their life story at the door, will not do that job for them.

I spoke of paying. Some supervisees, who are trainees or employees, may not pay you directly. Those who do pay may be embarrassed about money. It is often a taboo subject. So, when I raise my fees, or first negotiate them, I make sure that there is a chance for some talk about money. The counsellor has a chance to work out how much supervision she needs, whether she can afford it, whether her finances as well as other things make supervision in a group rather than one-to-one the best decision for her. In that conversation I am listening for her attitude to herself, in terms of money. Does she demand Nothing But The Best, in a way that seems impractical? Does she talk as if she is a pauper, though obviously well-funded? Is she ready to settle for anything I mention, without asserting her best interests? Is she more interested in getting what she calls her rights from her funding agency, than in the supervision itself? Alas, like me, you may recognise that one. Last-minute colds in the head and cars that will not start are in my experience strikingly more prevalent among those who are paid for than those who pay for themselves.

Not all, but a great many people who choose counselling as part or all of their work, seem comparatively uninterested in money. Certainly, if they were, they would be silly to take up a profession which is unlikely to make them anything in the way of a fortune. Since supervisors are likely to be of the same attitude, I think it is important not to collude in supervision at sliding uneasily round the taboos of fees and non-payments, and money generally. Discipline yourself to ask supervisees how they safeguard themselves financially. Many practitioners ask for payment some weeks in advance, always keeping themselves in credit with the client. As well as taking care of their peace of mind about having a regular income, this practice also prevents the client from using money to be punitive.

Many counsellors, though, work in voluntary settings. Sadly, I have noticed that clients who pay nothing for counselling, time and again attend irregularly, and in general seem to give less value to the counselling than those who pay. Given that we live in a very money-driven culture, I suppose this is not surprising. With children and young people who do not yet construe value in terms of money, what I have just been saying does not, mercifully, seem to apply.

TIME TO CHEW OVER: TIME TO CHOOSE

When people come to you for supervision, as part of a training, there can be a different and grave conflict about the sessions. It looks as if many people are like me, in hating to do what I have been ordered to do, even if it is demonstrably for my own good. This is the major weakness of all statutory education. It breeds resistance simply by being obligatory.

With all students, as with everybody I see for counselling, I take the precaution of insisting on a cooling out period at the beginning of our time together. When I told a psychiatrist about this device, he was to my surprise struck by what to him was the novelty of my invention. He was also flattering enough to say that he suspected that my use of it dealt with a vast part of the resistances that many professionals go on meeting in their clients for months or even years. That is my fanfare. Here is the device. You may have been using it yourself for years!

Before the end of the first session I have with a new supervisee or counselling client, I say that I would like them to go away and let a couple of nights pass, before telephoning me to say whether they would like to go on working with me. Commonly, they say that this is unnecessary, that they have made their minds up, that they want to get some dates fixed before their diary fills up, and so on. I stay with what I have said. The effect of this is that the client is absolutely clear in her own mind that she has chosen to work with me. For people whose style is blame or confusion, this is important.

Generally, I know by the end of the first session with anyone, whether or not I am prepared to work with them. So I communicate this. On occasion I know when we meet that I do not want to work with someone. Perhaps they turn out to be in some category of people I doubt I can be useful to. Whatever the reason, I need to say if I do not want to go on. This only happens rarely, because almost everyone telephones before a first visit, and the chances are that I can learn enough, as you can, in such a phone call, to let me decide.

From time to time I can feel the need of the cooling-out period myself. I feel dubious but unclear. I probably want to talk in my supervision about the person now sitting in front of me. In that case, I say that the cooling-off time is for both of us to make up our minds whether we want to work together.

Perhaps your supervisee works in a day centre or residential home where counselling is part of the service provided. Everyone who attends is assumed to have three meals a day and two group meetings a week and a counselling session, say. School counsellors, too, may have pupils sent to them by teachers. Encourage them too to make this time of reflecting available. I say this with some force, from the conviction that they undermine their effectiveness, working with people who have not decided for themselves on the sessions.

At one time I ran a weekly group for violent offenders, in a centre that was an experimental alternative to prison. When I and my co-worker were first there, we were hardly surprised to find that we had among us what P.G.Wodehouse might describe as some tough eggs in the back row. So we reminded them that they had signed an agreement to work at rehabilitation into ordinary life. We told them that the alternative was for them to go back to prison.

"Well, if you're going to twist my arm like that," said one, "I've got no choice, have I?"

"There is always choice," we said, if not in such crisp words, "and all choice involves consequences." It was hard work to make them see that they were to choose. We were not coercing. We were showing them their choice. They put effort into making all this our problem rather than theirs. They told us that their probation officers would be much nicer about it than that. They said that it would be on our consciences for the rest of our lives if we sent them to jail. I have often reflected gratefully, that they gave us an intensive advanced practical training in clear thinking and assertiveness.

This is certainly the most dramatic and immediate choice I have ever been in a position to point out to someone. What I am hoping to remind you is that there is always choice; but unless anyone is aware of having chosen to come and see you, you are setting off from a bad beginning. You need to guard against the woolly thinking of people who say that if one alternative before them is unpalatable, then they have no choice. This is a very common way of holding on to bad feeling, of grudge about the choice that is made.

If you are a school counsellor, you probably know all too well that despairing teachers can use you as a threat, and try to send pupils to you, as they might another time send them to the Head. The pupil who arrives like that is likely to be unco-operative, hostile, with all the liveliness and verve of a wet dishcloth.

This brings me to another practicality of the work of counselling and supervision, which is once more clearly ethical too. It is part of the job to let people know something of what they are in for if they come to see you. All practitioners train clients into their way of working. So long as they realise this and do it explicitly, they are likely to do it better.

The memory comes to me of a video of a client new to counselling being seen by a trainee Rogerian counsellor. The counsellor sat there silent with a Mona Lisa look on her face, which I guessed to be her way of imparting unconditional positive regard. It was certainly not getting through to the ever more nervous lady in the other chair, who obviously could not make head nor tail of the rather literal reflective statements slowly coming back at her.

"Aren't I talking loudly enough?" she asked at one point. She thought the counsellor was repeating her words for the counsellor's benefit, rather than as a means to her own enlightenment. What was missing was some exposition at the very beginning, of what the counsellor was assuming to be her role in the proceedings.

From time to time counsellors need to consider in supervision whether and how to write to clients. Many good practitioners express themselves indifferently on paper. As supervisor you will be exposed to many more letter-writing episodes than any one counsellor, so you have the possibility of becoming clear, fluent and gracious on paper. Encouraging such writing in your supervisees is important. An ill-phrased letter may undo a great deal of good work.

The commonest reason for writing to a client is when she has not come to one or more sessions. The chances are that the supervisee then feels grumpy and devalued. It is a moment for breathing deeply and finding some third eye rapport. The supervisor can usefully help the supervisee acknowledge the feelings she has. When she has dealt with them and moved into a suitable frame of mind you may together find a form of words for what needs to be written.

It is always possible that any letter sent in such circumstances is the last, or almost the last, communication there will be between the two parties. That is the proper context to start from. The supervisee needs to think through whether she wants to make this possibly last epistle a hymn of fury or blame, a reproachful guilt-inducer, or a clear negotiating statement about her present demands, the background of the demands, and her recognition of the client. The envelope will need to be marked Private.

Dear X,
I sat thinking of you when you did not arrive again on Tuesday, and remembered how often you have talked of mistrusting whether anyone cares for you. So I speculated on whether you were testing me a bit, and also giving yourself a bad time.
I thought too of the hard, and I think difficult, work you did the last time we met. In my judgement you have more to do, and it would be good for you to do it.
Do please leave a message on the ansafone to confirm your next appointment. I am keeping it open and will in any case charge you for it as we agreed.
I am also looking forward to seeing you.

The style of counselling must shape the letter style. This one is no more than an example of reasonable brevity, clarity, charity and assertion. The reader can see that the counsellor gave the client his time, even if he was not present. She neither blames nor rescues. She is not so formal as to sound bureaucratic.

I do not think it at all easy to write such letters, or the follow-ups, when no word comes back. But at times they are the last exercise of power properly open to the counsellor. The supervisor can encourage her to finish off her side of the counselling contract, by putting on paper what she still needs to communicate. A half-day spent writing letters, which will not be sent, to clients who have disappeared, is a good bit of supervisor and counsellor training, and one suitable for the occasional get-togethers of supervisors that I suggest at the end of this book.

PUBLIC RELATIONS

As well as being explicit within and about sessions, counsellors need to make themselves, and some hint of their way of working, known throughout any institution to which they are attached. At best, school counsellors occasionally take classes, and college counsellors take short courses, in which the values of counselling are demonstrated rather than just explained. Working out suitable interventions is one area where supervision moves nearer consultation, with some benefit.

Supervisees who are good at working in the small system of a pair or a therapy group, may not be much at ease in strategic thinking. In supervision you can work out a plan.

Offering a staff training group or support group can enhance co-operation through an institution. So can work on induction courses, or in any other training which appropriately shows counselling modes.

I remember the University Counsellor who took on the running of an induction week for new students. As well as group work and orientation to the campus, she taught them some ways of doing some of their academic work in pairs and small student groups. Then later in their careers she was in a good position to help them help themselves deal with exam panics, again by sharing tasks with peers.

In one comprehensive school the counsellor, at her supervisor's suggestion, set up a pastoral skills groups for the staff. Once a fortnight for two terms, large numbers of the staff stayed behind in the afternoons for a group event that they said did an enormous amount for their own good cheer, as well as making it easier to get on with their students.

In a certain commercial organisation the counsellor was appointed by the board, and the effect of this was to put the personnel department's noses out of joint. Supervision was needed even to diagnose this. Then the supervisor was able to encourage face to face approaches to members of the department, and finally their acceptance of her as a valuable member of the internal consultancy team in the organisation.

Another counsellor in an industrial concern was used more and more as listening ear by the chief executive. Then she began to suspect that she was being approached by other employees, not so much about their personal difficulties, but in the unacknowledged hope that she would relay their promotion hopes to the chief executive. After thinking it through in supervision, the counsellor talked to the chief executive. The outcome was that her post was re-defined as P.A. to that lady, and they all lived more comfortably ever after.

Whatever the setting, the supervisor needs to visualise her supervisee within it, and check that enough sensible steps are being taken to make a good working atmosphere. If the counsellor in an organisation is only a mysterious and slightly embarrassing or risible presence behind the sign on her door, the supervisor has work to do with her.

THE ECHO

Time and again, what goes on when a counsellor talks to the supervisor about a client, echoes part of what is going on between the client and counsellor, in their sessions together. If you have not been aware of this already, you will be, Oscar, you will. At first it may sound magical, or just unlikely, that the manner of the supervision can at times be a mirror of the counselling. Even people who are trained to work deliberately with transference, often in my experience overlook this aspect of it.

Since many more practitioners seem to get in a twist when asked to define transference, it is probably as well to put a sentence about it here. Like all truth, it can be described in simple language, and is no more than each person's transferring of their expectations in one scene in their life, to a different scene. The fun often starts when the other players in the second scene get dragged into these expectations, and even begin playing out some version of the drama role to which the dominant person has probably unknowingly assigned them.

For some reason many people seem to stick at the notion that transference is deep, difficult and somehow bad. Before deciding on that, you need to look at what it is about, and whether it is too much of a fixed idea.

If I am so convinced, say, that Men Are Bullies, then this transference, presumably from the early part of life, is not likely to make me much of a social turn-on. I am likely to cringe about, or get my bullying in first, and generally be the sort of character people roll their eyes about and avoid like the plague. My father was in fact a wise, an observant and deeply kind man. Looking back over my life, I can see how I have transferred my expectations of him on to some other men, who have tended to bring out that side of themselves with me, to the advantage of both of us.

In supervision, the echo or transference is magnificently informative, wherever it stems from. With the details of clients disguised, here are some examples of what I am talking about.

In one group I supervise, people have established a convention of spending the first few minutes of the meeting saying anything they need to get off their chests. Then they state how much time they each need, tailor their needs to reality, and, as they each begin, appoint their own monitor to remind them when their time ration is ending. Today Mary looked hot and bothered, and was unusually strident.

"It's no good," she said, with some defiance, "I'm absolutely desperate about G., and I've just got to have half an hour at least." Someone asked if she had brought a tape of a session.

"G. won't let me tape him", she pouted. John reminded her that he had agreed at the last meeting to bring a tape and notes about one of his clients to this one. He had been up till very late writing background notes which he had photocopied to circulate to everyone, and he was expecting to take at least an hour.

"Well in the end it doesn't matter if that waits till next week," said Mary, whining but seeming like someone who was certainly going to get her way. "I tell you, I just feel as if I shall explode if I don't get some help."

As Mary had never been so insistent in the group before, people agreed to give her her half hour first. She took some minutes growling and whining about G., who had obviously made her feel very frustrated. Then she described him, somewhat repetitively, and mostly in terms of his feelings. People had to ask her his age, work, who he lived with, how he was brought up. In that group, members generally gave such facts in a thumb-nail sketch at the beginning of a presentation.

"I know he needs help," she kept saying, "but there just doesn't seem to be any way of getting through to him."

"You sound as if you're trying too hard," said John. "Why don't you just stay quiet and let him run out of steam?"

"I've tried that, and he just talks and talks until I'm lost in what he's saying."

"He's frightened," said Paddy. "I bet he's too terrified to let you in. What sort of rapport have you tried to make with him?"

"How on earth can anyone establish rapport with Niagara Falls in the rainy season? That's what he's like."

Watching and feeling, trying to make sense of what was happening in the room, I saw how almost everyone responded to Mary's air of irritated desperation by producing, at considerable speed, Why-Don't-You? suggestions. It was as if they were feeding her good practice-serves in a metaphorical tennis game. She slammed every suggestion into the net. At last, nettled, someone said,

"I understand how difficult YOU'RE being. You've had forty-five minutes, and all that has happened is that we're all frustrated now."

I suggested that we spend even longer, to work out what was going on.

For a start, Mary had not appointed a time monitor, and nobody had pointed that out to her until this minute. In their turn, the rest of the group had seemed to enter into the spirit of things by suggesting, by giving advice, by interrupting, by making what looked like repeated attempts at cosy friendly control. Yet they were people who knew well that Mary had all the resources to work out her own solutions.

They reflected on what had gone on, and began to report images of the dialogue. The tennis game was one. Someone else said they had seemed like a lot of dithery maiden aunts trying to be helpful to a great bully of a nephew.

"Oh," said Mary, "G. was brought up by two maiden aunts. And he's fattish. I could imagine him being a bully."

"He bullies you." She accepted this.

The feel of the meeting had changed. We were once again a working group, a co-operative. Everyone took note that they could be magicked, black-magicked even, into a dialogue which everyone knew was useless, and which was a close re-enactment of the frustrating sessions with G. More than that, from Elsie's highly intuitive image about the dithery aunts, we were able to guess that the sort of exchange we had plunged into was one G. had been engaged in since early in his life. So we were contemplating two-stage magic. G. somehow converted Mary into his dithery aunt, or, more accurately, she took on that role with him.

Then, hey presto, she compounded the muddle and played G. when she came to talk about him, and we made a fair job of playing the aunts .

You notice that I asked group members for their images, their poetic rather than their rational intelligence about the scene we has acted out. This calling up of associations, of uncensored pictures, is specially valuable when you supervise a groups whose members are running groups themselves. Time and again, a simile, a fantasy, is a vivid clue to a bemused worker about what is going on in a counselling group where she feels she is not working to best effect. In the image she is likely to see the ways in which the group has perhaps been over-influenced by her mood and preoccupations, or by those of some other dominant member.

So, as well as everything else, supervision can be likened to a hill, where echoes of a counselling session, and echoes of the client's way of getting on with people, can clearly be heard if you listen out for them. The hill is not the counselling session. It is a place from which you can look back at it with a wider perspective.

The high art of supervising is to do with hill climbing, keeping an eye on the range of hills or triangles around the counsellor, and helping her scale them, from point to point. Then she will be able to see the landscape of her client's life, her own, the counselling itself, and the supervisory relationship, from different points of view than just her own. The next page expands this idea.

THE GEOMETRY OF COUNSELLING

Part of the job of supervising is to stay aware of the three points of a triangle, and make sure that the counsellor switches between them appropriately herself. There is the client's point of view, which may take in both his habitual attitudes, and whatever is likely to be going on for him in response to what the counsellor has or has not done there and then. There is the counsellor's point of view, in terms of her feelings, understanding and skills. And there is my point of view, as this person who is outside the two-person system, looking down from the top of the hill. The counsellor needs to be able to move to this position too. Patrick Casement refers to the Internal Supervisor who needs to be there throughout sessions. Richard Bandler talks of the Dissociated position, with much of the same meaning.

In this extract, notice the switches from viewpoint to viewpoint.

JANEY: *Um. Anyway, where was I? O yes. Um. This client of mine seems, er...*
ME: *What's going on? I'm ready to fall asleep!*
JANEY: *Sorry. I was a bit preoccupied.*
ME: *See if you recall what was preoccupying you.*
JANEY: *Different possibilities of what might really be going wrong for this client.*

ME: *I was starting to get indignant over here, as well as tired. I felt extinguished, put aside. I had the feeling you didn't notice I was here.*

JANEY: *That's just how he makes me feel.*

ME: *Then let's play for a few minutes with the idea that we've partly shuffled into each other's roles. You're playing him, and I'm playing you, emotionally. Tell some more about that preoccupation you mentioned.*

JANEY: *I felt doom-laden to the point of being, well, in a frozen panic. [She paused] Yes, maybe that is what I need to register. He is so stuck in terror and denying terror, that he will have very little attention free for noticing me.*

ME: *Tell me what you are saying about yourself, in saying that.*

JANEY: *[Laughs] O lumme, here I go again. Janey doesn't count.*

ME: *You see this client. I don't see him. So your judgement is very likely indeed to be better than mine about what you do when you are with him. But I want you to give me your impression at this moment of how stuck he really is, and how much he can cope with noticing you. In T.A. language, how much adult is available in him?*

JANEY: *Well of course, he does have rather a high-flying job.*

ME: *I was thinking of that. Yet anyone eavesdropping on us these last few minutes might get the impression he was about ready for custodial care! So you know that he can cope with the world very well in some ways. Are you still stuck in the echo effect with him, in an echo of how he influences many people to respond to him? Such a poor frail chap! You had better put up with being mesmerised to unconsciousness, or he will feel upset.*

JANEY: *Hm.*

Even if I had not been in imminent danger of joining Janey in what I call the echo, I think I would have been doing a better job in saying that I had got bored or sleepy or numb, than in pretending. If I spend my time as a supervisor trying to preserve a false image of myself, then it is possible that my behaviour will echo back into the counselling, as the counsellor copies me and does the same to her client. As the vast bulk of what brings people to seek counselling is to do with their difficulties in getting on with others, the least we practitioners can do is offer our own straightforwardness. They may not be in touch with their own.

You may have noticed that, though I began this chapter on the echo of the counselling session that often comes into the supervision room, other echoes are around too. I have just spoken of the echo that can, and I know often does, go back from supervision to the counselling. Then too, in the extract of the supervision with Mary, we came on the perhaps more obvious sort of echo: the client in the session echoes other scenes in his life.

In the picture, then, I put hills or triangles for the supervisor to keep in her awareness and bring back to the awareness of her supervisee. First there is the three person pattern of client, counsellor and supervisor. Then there is the triangle of transference. This is the client's movement between what I call:

The I-Thou of the immediate present in the room;

The general present of her preoccupations about partner, work, mortgages and other day to day subjects;

The third point is her early life and its shaping of her present attitude and responses.

At times the supervisor will do well to bring the counsellor's own triangle of transference into their conversation - and her own.

Those hills or triangles are rich mines of insight and potential change; there are plenty of them when you are dealing with one supervisee and one client. When you do supervision of group counsellors you are dealing with the whole of the Alps, with the Appennines thrown in for good measure. In my experience, this sort of supervision is more often done well in a group rather than one to one. Good workers will use the supervision group to speed their skills at letting the echo develop just enough to be recognised, and then pouncing before they are sucked into some storm or miasma which has little to do with them, and a great deal to do with the group under examination.

Perhaps the ideal for practitioners who work in counselling or therapy groups is to have some one-to-one and some group time in their supervision.

The last triangle in this geometry is another perhaps familiar to you, Transactional Analysis' Drama Triangle. This is the hideous configuration of Victim, Persecutor and Rescuer that most of us are more skilled at blundering into than in diagnosing. As you probably remember, the specially nasty bit of this triangle is that, once in, it is much easier to swap roles, and jump or slither between the three positions, than to bust the game by refusing to play.

As supervisor you may first get a whiff of this noisome configuration if you suddenly notice yourself lapsing for a moment into one of the roles. Do you suddenly feel more persecutory and blaming of your supervisee than seems in line with what she is saying? Or do silent aggrieved victim feelings begin to stack up in you, in relation to her and her client? Even more likely, do you suddenly notice that you are trying to rescue, by problem-solving for all three of you at once, or providing there-theres and other comfort to a counsellor who might do better to face that she is floundering with a particular client?

As a counsellor or as a supervisor, part of your work is to talk about what is going on unsaid between you and the person opposite. If you keep quiet about this emotional process, whether it is a change of pace or manner in the other, or your own responses to her and what she is saying and how you feel treated, then you lose effectiveness. You will do respectable, mechanical work, maybe. But you will leave out huge areas of potential learning for the person with you. And you will leave out risk and excitement and learning for yourself. To comment a process is to change it. Dare to blat!

To finish this subject here, I want to remind you of an important simplicity. Direct statements that start with I can be incontrovertible. They are about your experience, on which you are the world's only authority. Statements that start with you are often guesses. I come across people who remember this when they are counselling. Then as supervisors they go down, or bounce up, with acute bouts of the dread but often undiagnosed disease, Omnipotent Thinking, whose symptoms may include Second Sight and Alleged Infallible Accurate Empathy.

In the chapter on style there is more about which part of the system of supervisor-and-counsellor, or counsellor and-client, you comment. Whether or not you are self-disclosing, I suggest that the point of reference you need to acknowledge inside yourself, is what is happening to you in the moment. You may be playing echo to your counsellor's client's Grandad. You may be dragging the effects of last night's party into the session. You may be in a moment of clear recognition and synergy. If you fail to make a comment and enquiry, you may never know.

GETTING MOVING

The last chapter was mostly about some of what you need to remember to do in supervision. Now we can remind ourselves of some ways to enliven how we do that.

When a group of trainee counsellors filled in a questionnaire for me about supervision, an activity within sessions that most of them rated highly was role-play. I was not surprised. Any way of learning that involves some movement and imagination seems to me an improvement on just sitting on your bottom for the whole of a session.

In this chapter I shall describe a few ways, beyond the conventionally verbal, of working with supervisees. In case it is unfamiliar to you, I first give an example of one particular, and I think very effective way of setting up role play in supervision groups. Notice the tasks the supervisor does during it.

JO: *I've started seeing this couple, Larry and Lil, and I feel totally out of my depth. They seem to loathe each other and loathe me, and they interrupt the whole time. I can't honestly see why they come.*
After a little more talk, Jo decides that he would like a role play, as a way of giving himself more insight and grasp, and with luck some ideas for going forward. He picks Tom and Trish to play the couple, to which they agree.
SUP: *Place them and their chairs the way they tend to sit in the session. [HE PUTS TWO CHAIRS FOR THEM, FACING AWAY FROM EACH OTHER AT ABOUT FORTY FIVE DEGREES. GROUP MEMBERS LAUGH AND EXCLAIM]*

JO: *I've never even commented that to them, the way they won't look at each other. They walk in going hammer and tongs..*

SUP: *[I INTERRUPT] Settle for the role play, or have a good old winge. Not both at once. Which?*

JO: *Role play.*

SUP: *Start by standing behind Trish with your hands on her shoulders. Talk in the first person, describing yourself as if you are the wife, Lil. If Trish wants to find out more about Lil, she asks questions, also in the first person. Lil is the subject for the moment.*

JO: *My name's Lil. I'm 38. My father divorced my mother when I was two, and she married a man who didn't like me.*

TRISH: *Does my voice really sound like that?*

JO: *[HEIGHTENS HIS VOICE A LITTLE AND PURSES HIS MOUTH] I tend to shoot out a lot of words like a machine gun, then clamp my mouth shut. [KEEPING THIS STYLE, HE TELLS MORE ABOUT LIL, ALWAYS IN THE FIRST PERSON]*

TRISH: *What's my feel of myself, my underlying emotion?*

JO: *I feel pretty hard done by. Angry. I'd better fight my corner or I'll go down. [JO BREAKS OFF TO COMMENT] I hadn't sensed that properly before - the isolated feeling of having to keep lashing out or else be overwhelmed.*

SUP: *Remember, we're dealing with the Lil in you. That may be a very accurate guess. Or not. It's only a guess. Keep going.*

He and Trish work on in the same way for a few minutes, so that both have a fair sense of Lil as Jo sees or intuits her. Then he does the same exercise with Tom, cast as Larry. From time to time other people in the group ask questions of Jo-as-Larry or Jo-as-Lil. The questions are aimed to help Jo see more about his clients or his response to them. The questions are not merely to gratify the group member's curiosity. I make sure that all the questions are directly to the roles, so that a rambling About session does not set in.

NICK: *[TO JO WHO IS STANDING WITH HIS HANDS ON TOM'S SHOULDERS] Larry, does Lil have nice legs?*

TRISH: *[SUSPICIOUS] What do you ask that for?*

NICK: *I've a guess around sexual teasing in this marriage.*

JO: *You're right.*
SUP: *Talk in character; don't talk about.*
JO: *[AS LARRY] She's got film star legs. I like her to wear seamed stockings.*

You see how as this exercise goes on, Jo enlarges his sense of the people he is working with; other group members are involved and can add their enquiries; and Tom and Trish are learning a good deal about the characters they will role play in a few minutes.

Next, I ask Jo, Tom and Trish to imagine themselves in next week's counselling session. Notice that I do not ask them to go over the past, but to have a rehearsal of possibilities for the future.

Predictably, Tom and Trish soon have the bit between their teeth, and are galloping into virtuoso performances of the dominant couple, while Jo opens and shuts his mouth, much in the manner of an expiring codfish. I stop the scene as soon as I think the manner of it has really struck everyone enough.

Now another group member takes Jo's place, so he can sit and watch, instead of being out there as a protagonist. She soon flounders, at which point she says loudly, "Doubles all round!" In this group, this phrase has come to be the cipher to allow all group members to participate.

What they are now licensed to do is stand behind any of the characters in the role play, with hands on their shoulders, and speak whatever lines they deem it likely or important that that character utters. As soon as they have said their say, they sit down in the circle again.

Tom, Trish and Jo, or by now the counsellor who has taken his place, continue their dialogue, incorporating the statements for which they have acted as mediums. If the statements did not engage them, they carry on as they wish. In this way, much easier to do than to describe, a composite view of what is happening between Jo and his clients can be expressed and worked on in a direct experiment, rather than talked about. Some group members have an inkling of more of the subtext, the unspoken statements, under the couple's tart quarrelsomeness. Others have their own ideas of effective ways of intervening, and speak from the counsellor place.

The supervisor's job here has a little of stage director in it. It is up to her to interrupt creatively. Just letting a scene run down till people are tired and repetitive is usually much less useful than stopping whenever what looks like a telling point is made. When the role play itself is over, time is needed to let Jo, or whoever is seeking help, talk through some of his learning. He will need to reject some ideas openly, to question others, to remind himself where he easily falters or loses courage. In this talk afterwards, the experience of the other actors, and the rest of the group, is likely to be illuminating to Jo and to the members themselves.

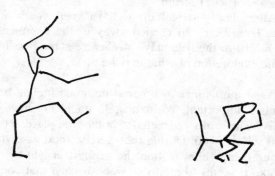

AND MY SKELETON WAS ARRANGED THUS.

Another stage directorial awareness is useful here too. I recommend that in any piece of role play, attention, which does not necessarily mean much time, is given to all the physical aspects of enactment like that I have just described, as well as to the compensating attitudes of the counsellor: in short, to the system which is physically portrayed by the two. Interrupt usefully, breaking off a scene, asking people to hold it or notice it, whenever you see matter for learning there to be commented, not just by you, but everyone present.

Ask the protagonist to sculpt or mime the attitude she could imagine herself to be in as she responded at that moment in the role play. Ask her to place someone else in the attitude she imagined her client to be in.

If there seems room for more awareness, you can next ask the person playing the client to sculpt the two from her stand-point.

Spectators, as in the old adage, often do see more of the game than the protagonists can; so their enactment of the body attitudes of the two may be yet more enlightening.

Reason is the camouflage of the emotions. Words are the symbolisation or the camouflage of attitude. Re-discovering that attitude is a short cut to truth.

After that you will do well to keep yourself and your supervisee from being so carried away in the comment that you forget to return to the role play to rehearse some possibility, or go on with the exploration of what may be done.

As at most times in supervision, good feeling between the participants is important. Without it, Jo might not have wanted to confess his feelings of incompetence in the first place, let alone with such open self-derision. During the exercise there is certainly quite lively group competition to find the deepest insight or the neatest intervention. It seems to me to work best when that competition is sensed by everyone to happen on a raft, a substructure, of good will towards Jo or whoever has put himself in a vulnerable position.

If you use role-play in training, you have probably notice that it is usually a licence to the id, or creative child, or whatever phrase you use to describe boisterous compensation for their good manners of other moments. If the people in the role-play do not allow for this exaggeration, they may scare themselves silly with the caricature representations they invent. They will wonder if they should even be working with a client who is so wild, so destructive, so stubborn, or so wily. The stage director skills of the supervisor are important here. She can point up when the emotional plague seems to be taking over, let people perhaps acknowledge and enjoy their indulgence, so they move beyond it to what looks more accurate intuiting of the people they are playing.

On occasion I have noticed that a group member who is not only very bright, but is a smart Alec, may produce excellent comment, which the group then ignores. There is something for the supervisor to comment, and for everyone to learn at such moments, about hostility and resistance. Most of the time, the group works far more effectively if love and co-operation, as well as hostility and competitiveness, are openly present and recognised.

THE VIGNETTE

Very often a piece of role play supervision is best ended with a vignette. From what the supervisee has learned, she sets up a final short scene in which she reminds herself once more of a new possibility, a way of breaking an old habit, or whatever has salience for her at that moment.

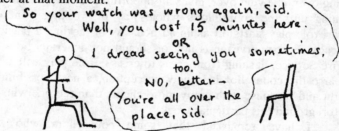

Role play in one to one supervision cannot be of just this kind. The only combinations available are that the supervisor plays client, or counsellor, with the supervisee taking the complementary roles. Both these exercises make for vividness and change of pace, and generally advance learning. My practice is, if we use role play, usually to take the part of the client first. I shall certainly know enough already about the client I am playing, not to need a formal hands-on-shoulders introduction like the one I suggested for group supervision. From the client place, I can see for myself just where the counsellor falters, or where, perhaps, she is doing fine but misdoubting herself. I am sometimes less willing to play the counsellor, particularly with supervisees I suspect of laziness. I do not want to hand them a set of ready-made interventions to carry away and serve up to their client, irrespective of what that poor person is thinking and talking about. I have known such things happen.

By and large, if a supervisee says in a wistful or wheedling voice that she would so like to know what I would say in this or that circumstance, I take care not to oblige. On the other hand, working with competent counsellors who have come across an old blind spot of their own, or a client whose behaviour they are not yet making sense of, I let myself play counsellor for a two or three-minute demonstration that we can then talk over.

Both are important, the experiment and the time for reflection. The role play may give an immediate insight. The talking over, chewing over, gives an opportunity for assimilating the learning into the counsellor's whole way of working. In other words, role play starts off as an ad hoc way of tackling a particular difficulty. But supervision is not, or should not generally be a kind of Fire Service, dashing from crisis to crisis. Role play will at best rehearse the counsellor in a new perception, a new possibility of insight and response with many more clients than the one who is in the foreground this particular week.

I have remarked that some counsellors who were unfamiliar with role play until they came to supervision with me, have then marched off and set their clients to role play in counselling sessions. The instances that have come back to me have sounded a creative way of letting the client find out or underline something for herself, sometimes at a moment when the counsellor confessed to me that she had to bite back an impulse of her own to advise or moralise.

Another way of allowing a direct experiment, a rehearsal or dry run, in supervision, is to use objects to stand in for people. Perhaps the most familiar way is to let the counsellor speak to an empty chair or cushion, as if they were occupied by the person she is talking about. Then she can change places, and reply to what she has just said, from the other person's stand-point, or rather, sitpoint. If you have not tried doing this, you may feel sceptical of such an awkward and artificial device. As most people who have tried it will tell you, it very often leads quickly to enhanced insight about the effect of each person on the other, and of the subtext, the emotional dialogue that has been going on between them below the words. It is direct a way as I know to let the supervisee experience the other point of the triangle, the client's.

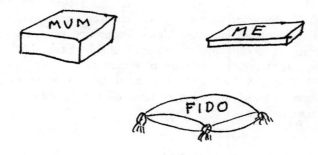

STAYING LIVELY

Creating liveliness in supervision is not merely agreeable; it makes experience vivid, and helps most people to remember clearly what they have learnt. As well as role play, there are many other methods to help you to freshness and attentiveness. In P.N.E.U. schools, I remember, they allege that children's attention span is at best around twenty minutes. Unless something very absorbing is happening, I doubt that grown-ups reliably have much longer attention, for working in any one particular way.

You may well have invented devices of your own. Here are some more of my ways of bringing variety into supervision from time to time.

TAPES FOR TOTAL RECALL

Sound and video tapes are used almost exclusively by some supervision teams. To my mind tapes are about fifty per cent miracle and fifty per cent curse. The curse is partly just the technology. The damn things do not work consistently well. Sometimes they refuse even to start. The quality on them can be so appalling as to make play-back a penance. Tapes click loudly and run out in the midst of a delicate piece of work, leaving anxiety about whether to stop everything in order to attend to the machine rather than the person opposite. They are voluminous, and take far more time to riffle through than does a written transcript.

All these are physical objections. Far graver are the ethics of taping. A compliant client may well agree to taping, but really feel thrown off balance by the sense of being recorded. Much more than any other records, tapes are incontrovertible evidence. They are the blackmailers' friend, exposing every word, and on vision-tape every gesture, to whoever picks up the cassette and plays it.

In a CCTV Ethics Group in London University, we made a strong case for never allowing a tape of any counselling session to survive that session. The counsellor then has the opportunity of playing back the words uttered, to a client who tends to forget or deny what she has recently said. On vision-tape, the client can monitor her own fidgets or any other mannerism, during the session. At the end, the counsellor can deal with all the client's anxieties about the violation of privacy, by requesting her to push whatever button is necessary to wipe the tape. Making this a routine is likely to encourage clients to use taped play-back enthusiastically.

During training, you are very likely to have used taped sessions of peer counselling as tuition and supervision material. I feel cautious about doing even this. An ethos can drift into this practice, in which students feel too embarrassed to say that they do not want themselves to appear as clients in this way. Then they may become so wary in their peer-counselling sessions, that little development is possible. If very strict confidentiality bounds are agreed and held to for the tapes, people may feel freer to do the vivid learning that tape makes possible.

Without doubt, from the narrow but important viewpoint of supervision and the counsellor's development, tapes are a most excellent aid. Some of my supervisees occasionally bring along the tape of a session in which they have counselled a colleague, who is probably known to me. On occasion, both have been in the room together when we have gone through such a tape, and good learning for both seems to have resulted.

Other counsellors persuade clients from time to time to allow taping, for the purposes of supervision. Sometimes I get the counsellor to ask the client to mark the cassette in a way she can recognise. Then in time the tape can be returned to the client, either verifiably wiped, or for her to wipe. I know that there would have been opportunity for copying the tape in the meantime. But this somewhat laborious procedure usually makes the point that it is meant to: that the counsellor and the invisible supervisor are concerned about the client's privacy.

Given that by one means or another a counsellor arrives at supervision with a tape to deal with, you are faced with perhaps fifty minutes of material. I ask the supervisee to edit the tape heavily before she arrives, and if possible bring her own play-back machine, so that the inconsistencies on the counter of my machine and hers do not waste our time. In the editing, she is to limit herself to an agreed amount of play-back, usually adding up in total to no more than about twelve minutes. The rest of the time is for her and my comment.

We may be reviewing a session simply to see in a general way how the counsellor is working. In this case, I probably ask her to mark two or three interchanges where she feels pleased with herself for what she achieved. As well, she will point up some places where she is less sure of what she has done. As you may guess, most counsellors seem more eager to point out their possible shortcomings, than to underline their successes. So this discipline is designed to improve their perspective on their work. It may with luck remind them too to allow their clients to discuss more than problems and difficulties, and to notice the ways in which they are coping successfully.

When workers bring me pre-edited tapes, they make notes beforehand as well. Sometimes they send these in before the session, and I have had a look or listen by the time they arrive. Unless I am paid to do it, I should not like to listen to complete tapes, with all the pauses, inaudible lumps and other grey areas that may well be recorded. It is not in any case my job to make a complete evaluation. The counsellor much more usefully does that for herself, and then checks her findings with me or you later on.

PERFORMER IN CONTROL

Sometimes you can get a good impression of your supervisee's work by letting her play back an unedited part of a session, with her finger on the pause button. Again, this is a method that is used very extensively in some training. I like it sometimes. She stops the tape whenever she sees or hears something she wants to comment. You can run the tape back to retrieve moments you want to talk about, if she has omitted them. This method shows not only what goes on in the session, but also a glimpse of the internal supervisor in your supervisee, as she critiques what she has done.

THE COMPOSITE COUNSELLOR

In the last chapter I spoke briefly of doubling. By this I meant, standing behind someone with your hands on their shoulders, for as long as it takes to utter what you want them to say. If you have not tried doing this, you may wonder about the point of it. The best way to find out is just to experiment. What I like is the economy of this way of working. Rather than have another member of the supervision group go through some lengthy and possibly offensive preamble, such as, "Well if I was you I'd want to say..." or, "Why haven't you told him...?" , the supervisee simply hears the content of an alternative intervention.

In group supervision I use this method very often. It is a way of simulating the discipline of a counselling session, in which the words uttered by the counsellor need to be clear, few and useful. It is tougher to stand and pretend to make an actual counselling intervention, than to loll back in a chair playing the grand old fireside game of "Haven't you tried?" It is an exposing and challenging exercise that supervisees learn from quickly.

THE TRIANGLE

From time to time in this book I have brought up the idea of the triangle of Counsellor, Supervisor and, [for the sake of a different

*initial], Patient. This exercise works directly with this triad, I use it
in groups which split into threes, and even with pairs of supervisees,
with me as third figure. Each person in the three takes on the role
of C, S, or P. The counsellor usually begins in the C position, and
responds to questions from the other two. These questions aim to
help the supervisee understand more about herself and her client,
and move on from whatever difficulty has made her ask for
attention. For example:*

S: What sort of rapport have you with P?
*P: What's your private judgement about how I use these
sessions?*
*When everyone feels ready, the supervisee moves to the client
position, P, and the others switch roles and question her again.*
C: What are you really wanting from me?
S: Tell me what your counsellor is like.
The last shift puts the supervisee in the supervisor position.
C: Give me your criticisms of what I have been doing.
*P: Was my anger last session a transference phenomenon? Or
was it mostly to do with my train being cancelled?*

I am very fond of this exercise. Everyone is engaged in the
work. People rise to the subtlety required, and regularly produce
questions of great appropriateness. Time and again I find that
more has been elicited and explored than if I had been the only
person responding. All players tend to report insight about their
own way of working, gained from intervening in this way on
someone else's work.

As I described at the end of the chapter on role-play, to
my mind much of what is said in a counselling session is likely to be
a verbal way of symbolising underlying emotionality, which is
attitude. Anything I can do to cultivate in supervisees a habit of
imagining their and their client's attitude from moment to moment
as they work, is likely to help their effectiveness.

The client may apparently be talking about her attitudes
and responses in the rest of her life. You as an experienced

counsellor are aware of how what she says connects to the present, to what is going on between you and her. All this applies as clearly, in my opinion, to supervision.

ATTITUDES
To make all this more vivid, I like from time to time to invite a supervisee to stop talking, and make a tableau of her and me at that moment, so that she notices the temporary system we have invented. Then I may respond with my picture of our tableau, or our wordless mime.
Or I can ask her to set up what she imagines my version of the tableau would be.
Anyone else present may want to chip with another sculpt, which to her mind represents what is going on emotionally in the little system in front of her.
Once people have grasped this idea, the latent caricaturist or cartoonist in them is likely to emerge to useful effect.
When you and they have seen this tableau, there is sometimes much to be gained from asking the counsellor to imagine and then demonstrate what tableau would be more satisfactory. If you agree with her, you can look for ways to achieve it between you.

This can be a way of nipping a collusion in the bud, or revealing some antagonism we have not noticed or admitted. The method is vivid, economical of time, and lets in some of what might be screened out of words. After all, as a species we had an enormous number of generations with vestigial speech, before we became the over-fluent word-bandiers we can be now. We have the equipment to recognise and infer our attitudes to each other without re-symbolising them into speech.

Experiment, if this idea is new to you. The feeling is of using a different part of the mind in doing so. Tableaux reach the parts only words cannot reach.

USING PROPS

*Another device which supplements or replaces some words in
supervision, has a small overlap with play therapy. Specially in one
to one sessions, I sometimes suggest that the supervisee uses some
of the shells and pebbles in a bowl on the table near us, to show her
version of some scene she is describing.*

*Denise came to me·one day with an involved story of the various
agencies a new client was in touch with. I began to be lost in the
complexity of the story, and said so. Denise said the same had
happened to her when she was with Anne, her client. She fetched a
pile of books from the shelf, and began to build what looked like a
version of Stonehenge on the floor. In the middle she put a paeony
to represent Anne. I asked what all this was about, not sceptically,
but with considerable interest. Denise was concentrating hard, and
I trusted that she was finding things out for herself.*

*"Yes," she said with conviction, looking at the scene. "This is how
Anne's world sounds to me. A series of little shelters that she
dashes in and out of." I asked where Denise was in the scene.
Interestingly, she had forgotten herself. Anne was so busy and
earnest that Denise had somehow let herself be tuned out, except as
a worried observer. So the sculpt was useful in leading to more than
one insight.*

*Now I asked Denise to use the books or whatever else she needed
from round the room, to set up a picture of how she would like to
have her counselling with Anne develop. After a moment, she put
the books into two parallel lines. "Too many bolt-holes," she said
darkly. "Anne goes from the F.S.U. to Social Services to the
Tavistock to this charity thing to Samaritans to the community
counselling service to a private therapist to the doctor. No! Next
time I see her I shall show her my picture of all this. And I'll give
her the choice. See me OR keep running around. Not both.*

THE TRIANGLE PERCEIVED

*People learn best when the learning model presented to them
resembles, or easily adapts to, those they set up in their own minds.
I keep talking about the Triangle. To some people it is on the flat,
a plan, perhaps with equal sides. To others it will immediately
translate in their minds to an elevation, with the supervisor literally
in an overview position. Getting supervisees to imagine and describe
or even draw their, possibly varying perceptions of this triangle, is a
greater aid to communication than it might seem. I remember one
supervisee who placed the supervisor almost beside her, and found
this an encouraging configuration. Another had me in the same
place, but with images of me breathing down her neck and cramping
her style. Until she had put me where she wanted to in a drawing,
she did not free herself to be in a useful dialogue with me in reality.*

*In the same way, let people take a moment to visualise the sort of
links or lack of them they see between the three points of the
triangle.*
*The supervisor too can learn a great deal for herself from noticing
how she is seeing, and how using, the triangle.*

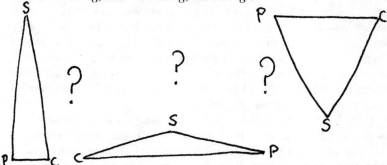

*Different supervisees on different days will need different emphases.
Overall, I hope you will agree, much of our work as supervisors is to
encourage her to move flexibly in her imagination between all those
points. The better we are at doing that ourselves, the clearer the
learning we offer.*

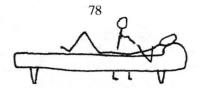

SKIN RELATION

Many practitioners get themselves in a twist from time to time about touching. They and their clients are likely to be inhibited in different ways. Much of what I say here about clients is likely to apply at least in part to counsellors too. As supervisor you will do well to encourage your supervisees to both confidence and discretion on this literally touchy subject. Most ractitioners acknowledge its importance. Their social and professional training may not have helped them, as you can, to be clear. Do they want to reflect general norms about touching? Do they want to make a cultural shift? Those are the choices. As supervisor you can help them remember the remarkable importance of physical handling.

I remember Harlow's experiments with monkeys, specially that in which young monkeys were exposed to wire netting mother-shapes which contained perfectly good milk, and cloth mother shapes, similarly equipped. It took that experiment to remind many people of what the rest had always intuited - that monkeys, and probably people, respond far better to some comfort and warmth than to coldness and discomfort.

Very many of the people who turn up for counselling have been through some version of the wire-netting monkey experience. Yet you as counsellor may well be chary of turning into no more than temporary cloth mothers for them. My mind is running on animals. I think of the pleasantness of having a cat sit on my knee, and the uncomfortable reflection that goes along with that; by stroking and cuddling cats, we literally infantilise them. They act like kittens, asking for fondling and grooming, because we step in right where their mothers left off, and keep them for the rest of their lives as part-baby. It is possible to do something like that with humans.

Conversely, I remember a recent and pitiful set of experiments with chimpanzees, in which the young were variously deprived of contact. Those kept away from their mothers completely for a certain period became totally anti-social, responding to all attempts at contact with attack, and generally behaving like juvenile delinquents. Autopsy showed a withering of part of their brain. The inference is that something as drastic probably can happen to humans. What is emotional is physiological too.

Such are our powers, however, shown in the extraordinary recovery people sometimes make after brain damage, that it is worth, in my view, assuming that re-learning of love, of social behaviour and its pleasures is possible.

What makes me speak at such length of all this is in part as a reminder of the enormous effect people have on each other, every moment, when we are in, and when we are apparently out of, contact. The contact the client has with you as a counsellor, and that we have as supervisor and counsellor, undoubtedly and demonstrably have direct measurable physical effects on us all. Physical. I am not talking just in some vague area of vibes and fancies, but directly of body chemistry: of health.

There are schools of counselling which favour a certain remoteness in the counsellor. At worst this can be wire-netting relating - offering excellent milk, in the form of correct diagnosis and comment, but modelling the emotional starvation which has perhaps characterised the client's world for much of his or her life. At the other end of the scale are those whose practitioners sometimes behave as if smiling, cosy, smother-mothering or daddy-hugging constitute helpful behaviour. At worst this manipulates the client being a domestic cat, or else into getting-better-for Daddy or Mummy, or feeling bad for failing to. It induces dependent feelings beyond the real dependence there is in the relation between counsellor and counselled, or supervisor and supervised.

The social taboos and fears around touching are all, insofar as I have traced them with many people, to do with sex and violence. When I am working as a counsellor, I rarely touch people during a one-to-one session. Often I put a hand on their arm as they leave. Touch seems to me so potent that I do not want to rouse the amount of hope or of fear, or the impulsive responses, or the suppressed impulses, that might result. I feel shy of touch, one-to-one, with people who have come to me because they are not feeling as put-together as they want to.

In a group I feel and behave differently. The presence of other people seems to help make clear that I am not making serious sexual advances to someone when I touch their hand or head or whatever. And the presence of other people also assures me that I am not likely to be swiped by the person touched, who may associate intimacy and violence, to the point of panic response. In a group, I may touch a number of people at different times. So it is clear that I am not setting up an exclusive pairing with anybody. One to one, this would not be demonstrable.

But social mores are changing, mercifully. Crying is far less derided among men than was true twenty years ago. Holding therapy for autistic children has been shown on television. Little by little, I imagine, people who spend more of their working hours dissociated from physical contact, sitting at their lonely computer terminals, will balance this alienation with more literal ways of being in contact, than just keying in to databanks. They will look for dance and movement and sitting close, and generally being in touch with other humans. I supervise people who range from never-touching through to always-touching in their work. At another extreme, some spend much of their therapy or counselling sessions in movement, and use far fewer words than I do.

So, is there a right and a wrong? As a supervisor you need to know both what is right for you, and where you are tolerant of other people's practice, and where your own scare gets in the way of accepting different methods from your own.

The only rules I have come up with for myself are the same as in other aspects of supervision. I require honesty of the counsellor. From time to time a supervisee reports to me that a client asked for some physical contact which she gave, though knowing she did not want to. That is not honest.

EMMA: *He stuck out his hand and said he wanted me to hold it the way his grandmother used to.*
ME: *I'd like to see how that happened.* [SHE STUCK HER HAND STRAIGHT OUT, FIXED MY GAZE, AND TOLD ME TO HOLD THE HAND. I AT ONCE DID NOT WANT TO, JUST AS SHE HAD] *Now switch over. I'll stick my hand out, and you find a different response.* [I COPIED HER ACTIONS, AND SAW HER LEAN FORWARD, LOOKING TORN BETWEEN OBEDIENCE AND DISTASTE]
EMMA: *I want to respond as if you're him, because a memory just came to me. Mr X, you told me in our first session that you are used to getting your own way. I'm finding it difficult not to do as you tell me, without considering my own feelings. I'd prefer you to put your hand down.*
ME: [GUESSING HOW HE MIGHT ANSWER] *You're side-stepping.*
EMMA: *I'm looking for how to be useful to you. You once told me you wanted to look at how you handle people. Find a different way now.*

It had not taken long for Emma to see that her client was probably intent on rather literally getting the upper hand with her, as he said he did at work. Not touching at that moment might lead to more learning than a dishonest response could.

More complicated, to my mind, is the sad client who wants comfort. When someone I know already has arrived at a session with the news of the death of a child or other close friend or relative, I have sometimes felt much more useful to that person and myself, in simply holding them and letting them cry. Then with others, who are not in a particular crisis, I have suspicions that their low feelings are a victim racket, aimed at making me rescue them from reality. I become much more interested in the structure of what is going on between us than in obeying the requests made to me. I am more concerned with finding out why they want to cast me as cuddler, than in doing any cuddling.

My relation with them, after all, is bounded very clearly by time and money. Maybe I have only spent four or five hours in their company, ever, at that point. Are they trying to turn me into The One Person Who Really Understands? Are they inviting me into collusive beatification? Help. Perhaps I shall be of more real use to them if I show them my boundaries, and prevent them oozing into parent-child or lover-like relating with me.

So, the few rules I can think of about contact are

Never initiate contact without checking in words if it is all right to do so.

If invited into physical contact, find your honest response and talk about it, whether it is a yes or no, whether you have a hug or just sit there. Relate what is going on to other parts of the client's life than just this moment.

Slip outside yourself for a half-second and look at the system. What do you look as if you're doing, from the internal monitor or supervisor position? What do you look like from the client's position?

Talk about the contact. Keep it in the foreground rather than having it as an apparently ignored activity.

Much of what I have said here is in the context of therapy itself. With many of the supervisees I see, who are working alone a great deal, I let myself kiss them or hug them in greeting and farewell, and feel the better for it. I also check with them whether they are transferring this way of going on to their clients, and whether they feel that that is proper.

I do not have any axe to grind about making you hug your supervisees. You may roll your eyes to heaven at the thought. Well, see what that is about. Check that you are not covertly training them to coldness. If not, then all seems fine.

Some of my supervisees justify physically showing their good feelings to their clients, with some of the arguments I have used in relation to them. People who come to counselling are often at a vulnerable transition in their lives. Reminding them of the simplicity and economy of effort in an embrace is good modelling. Well, I am not out to convert supervisees to do all the same things that I do. But in this as in any other exchange, I ask the supervisee to check whether she is helping the client into being better at living, or whether she is setting up the Garden of Eden, and making the counselling sessions a substitute for life, for the client, and even for herself.

The splitters, the people Melanie Klein perceived so vividly, can have a great time with a counsellor who will join in with a game of being all-good or all-bad. That gives the splitter a chance to cast her spouse, family, maybe the rest of the world, in an opposite role. In such a case the counsellor is aiding the client into building unreality.

I often feel suspicious of physical contact in counselling which is not acknowledged in words. If a client wants a hug from my supervisee, then the supervisee knows that she is not violating that person's kinosphere in giving it. But I want her also to ask the client, "Who else do you hug? Who hugs you?" I want her to critique the hug. One hug can be a complete dissertation on how that person gets on with people. Is she a flopper on to your shoulder, a clinger who won't let go? Is she stiff as a board, snatching you to her upper half for a second, then pushing you off? Does she go in for an enveloping writhe that results in you feeling sexy? What feelings does she give herself as she hugs you? There is a great deal to find out about a hug, or anything else, if the counsellor is encouraged to do her job properly, and actually notice and comment what goes on in the session, as well as join in with it.

As I write this chapter, I imagine looking at it again in ten or twenty years time. I shall be content if it seems quaint and out of date, because people have returned to greater easiness than most of us have now about touching each other. If Victorian values win, however, then I suppose that touch will still for many people be fraught with sexual unease, and, alas, what I have written may still apply.

THE ANNUAL REVIEW

Many counsellors build into their work an occasional review session, when with their client they look back at what they have done or not done, and forward to what they might tackle next. These people are likely to understand the usefulness in supervision too, of this deliberate critical look. This section is about ways of setting up and using such a review, as supervisor and supervisee.

The first step is to moot the idea, and set a time for discussing it. If you rush straight into the discussion, the counsellor is at a disadvantage: you have already been brooding about the subject; that is why you raised it. She has probably thought about it a good deal less. She may need time to know whether she is scared at the idea, hostile to it, and in danger of bad faith compliance with you.

When you do discuss it, what needs to be decided is

When
What for
How

It might be easy to think that the What For is implicit in the task of review. Rather than jog along on that assumption, make space for you both to talk about what you might get out of doing it. Is the review all to be about the counsellor? Is there to be mutuality, with talk too about how you are doing as supervisor? Are you going to give space to thinking about specific further training? Will you make an opportunity for changing how supervision happens in future? You may be a wonderful supervisor; but in terms of career development, would your supervisee do well to think about trying a different person, perhaps from a different discipline, or the opposite sex?

The What For gives proper importance to the context of the counsellor's work. This may on some occasions usefully extend to looking at how far her practice is in line with her philosophy. Another time, it might be about how she is living her life at the moment, and whether counselling is still the proper work for her. If she is in therapy, she may not need to do this. But many counsellors have no other professional to talk to than you. The What For may therefore once in a while take in thinking about a career change.

At best, the review can be a very exciting occasion, for taking a large view, and making new plans. For each review to be effective, the counsellor as well as you as supervisor need to know your answers to the What For.

The How can also be expressed in some reminder questions, including

> *Who is going to write something?*
> *What is she going to write?*
> *What is going to be done with the writing?*

Years of being school children have lodged in us the model of teacher writing a report, which we wait, probably trembling, to see torn from its envelope by a parental figure. If anything about this way of starting the review appeals to you, then a variant is to ask the pupil to write a similar report about teacher. In other words, if you write about your supervisee, she writes about you. Then if you wish you can both go through the envelope-opening experience, and read the reports through before you meet to talk through what has been said.

This appeals to me a good deal less than its opposite, which is to have the supervisee write a report on herself, which she submits to the you, either beforehand, or when you meet to discuss the contents. As you will not need to be reminded if you have done such a thing, writing a report on yourself, which is to be talked over with another, albeit friendly, person, is a great deal more challenging than sitting around and simply uttering a few items of appropriate self-criticism, which can easily be chucked back into the trash-cans of your mind if they feel uncomfortable.

From this you gather that I am in favour of doing some writing, rather than having just a verbal exchange. Selective amnesia is the enemy of such talk. On many occasions I have observed how people manage to jettison into some unlit corner of their minds, the shrewd, kindly, well-worded and useful descriptions of them that are made by themselves and others in conversation.

On a counselling course where I lectured, we used the device of having each of a group of ten people take turns once a year to sit in the hot seat, and hear back one sentence that each other person present needed to say to them.

Most students promptly forgot whatever praise or appreciation was voiced, and held on to any piece of carping, whether it seemed very relevant or not. A few did the opposite, and managed not to hear overt or implicit complaint or criticism. The one rescuing statement put in by some tender-hearted or hypocritical peer would be all they chose to keep available to consciousness.

The exercise became far more effective when we asked the person on the hot seat to appoint a scribe, who wrote down the statements for her. If she wrote for herself, that too seemed to take away from the occasion, by keeping her out of contact with the speakers. Later she made a fair copy for herself of these notes, and at the next meeting was asked to make some comment on them, in the same group. In this way we incorporated a form of Telling Back, which is a most effective reinforcer of learning, into the exercise.

What makes me spell this out so completely, is to remind you of the possibility of using a form of the same exercise as a supervision review, if you are dealing with one person or a group who are reluctant to sit at home by themselves to do their writing. If you are in a group, take care to remind the person in the hot seat that she too is a member of the group, and needs to add her own comment about herself to those of the others. Unless this happens, you are back with a spoken version of the school report.

Perhaps you were like me as a school child, and often chose the path of psychological interpretation to defend myself against unwelcome judgements. "Well Miss Evans is a pig. She says nasty things about everyone." "He only put that because he knows I'm a lot cleverer than he is. He just wants to put me down." I found ways of wriggling away from responsibility for statements I did not much fancy. If the person in the hot seat keeps silent, she may manage to do something of the same kind.

If the person being judged adds her own judgement, she has the opportunity to think in a properly critical, rather than just a defensive way, about herself. One of two outcomes is likely. Either she will say something of value to herself; or she will be inappropriately defensive. In the latter case, if she is in a group of counsellors who are competent enough to be practising at all, she

will be sussed. The occasion may become a little nerve-wracking; it will also be an excellent reminder to everyone present of how to deal with someone who is being avoidant. It will be an implicit piece of training for counselling, as well as an important task in its own right.

As may have occurred to you already, many of the devices I suggest here for a supervision review, may be adapted by the counsellor for any review sessions she has with a client. In the same way, you may have methods of reviewing with your counselling clients, that will work too with supervisees.

In individual supervision there are still ways of making some of whatever writing there is to be, take place at and after the review session, rather than before it. Both people may want to make a few notes before their meeting. Then together they talk their way through their formal or informal agenda, of which I shall speak later.

Once again, it may be valuable to have each make notes for the other person, rather than herself. Then in private, both write up an expanded version of these notes, to present and discuss next time they meet, with a view to altering them if necessary, to produce a document that both people agree. This part is important. There is sometimes an amazing difference between what I think someone has taken as the spirit and letter of a discussion, and what they put on paper about it afterwards.

Though I tell supervisees not to expect their clients to understand them all the time, I can still be surprised that communication can falter just as much in supervision.

In training, most people who go in for this profession respond gratefully to the injunction to be open to self and open to others. That ethos stays with most supervisees. Then here and there I find good practitioners who grow a little defensive, over used to their own well-tried methods and assumptions. The review is a way of licensing a bit of healthy boat-rocking.

These wry remarks apply with just as much force to supervisors, who may get particularly used to hearing themselves hold forth to younger people, who possibly give them even a shade more reverence than they deserve. Hence my enthusiasm for making the review a two-way affair.

WHAT TO TALK ABOUT

The widest trawl is perhaps the impressionistic exercise I spoke of earlier in this chapter. In a group of more than a very few people, there is a good chance of achieving a useful picture of any member by no more than inviting people to say what they need to say to her, in the context of her as a counsellor.

The opposite end of the spectrum is to procure one of the many performance scales popular in management circles, adapt it to counselling, and let the supervisee mark herself and or you on ratings of one to ten on a series of abstractions, such as clarity, attentiveness, concern, or whatnot. To my mind this is a somewhat airy-fairy exercise, even though it leads to rows of figures that look splendidly mathematical and irrefutable. If the supervisee is prepared to ask some of her clients to fill in the scales too, she may arrive at a more useful read-out. What is most important is to use such an exercise as the basis of a discussion which leads to action.

What are you and she going to do less of and more of?

How will you set that up?

How will you monitor yourselves?

This is as good a place as any to state my belief that any review which does not have a recognisable and monitored effect on future behaviour, might as well not take place. A review is not about the bolstering of complacency, nor yet about the tidy apportioning of blame. It is about a co-operative look at what has been, is, and can enjoyably and usefully be in the future.

As I mentioned earlier in this chapter, a creative way in to the review is to consult your supervisee about what she sees as the most valuable method, and the most valuable focus, for her.

As part of the exercise, she may for example decide to take one of her counselling sessions, and go through it in detail, rating herself on some such system as John Heron's Six Categories of Intervention. Doing this produces more than an appearance of hard data. It will show her and you just how much she interrogates, confronts, and so on. It can be a sound basis for planning next year's development. Or she may ask you to view one of her sessions through two-way mirror or on tape. In other words, she is quite likely to come up with ideas that you have not thought of, and from which you both benefit.

Whatever the form of the review, you need within it in some way to let the following questions be answered. They may be considered in relation to the counsellor, and as well in relation to you who are looking to supervise her the best way you can.

What do I want more of, less of and maintained?

What do I want the same, more of, less of from you?

What have I achieved?

What have I not done that I wanted to?

What are the stoppers?

What do I want to do next?

What needs to happen so that I can?

What do I need from you to help me?

How shall we know when we've got there?

How shall we monitor as we go?

When?

As well as some mutuality, as I have already stressed, I see it as proper that most of the attention is on the counsellor's work, and on how she gets on with the supervisor. If the supervisor, as I hope she will, wants an exhaustive review for herself, I doubt if she should try to get it in the time the counsellor is paying to have with her. I hope that comment shows how I see the bulk of the time of the review being focussed.

The first question gives space for a wide look at how the counsellor sees herself doing her job. The next lets her give her view of the supervisor. The later ones only apply if the counsellor wants to make some alteration in her way of working. If she does not, then I am a bit alarmed. Innate scepticism keeps me from supposing that you are supervising the Perfect Counsellor.

The last three questions are designed to give reality to what at the time of the review can only be ideas. I remember one counsellor who at her review told me that she had time and money for some more training, but was not clear in just what area. We worked out a kind of shopping period, of the summer months, when she would go on various short courses. Then we set a date in our diaries for talking over where she was getting to.

I emphasise the usefulness of taking out your diaries at a review session, and marking a date or dates when you will look at progress on the counsellor's change of intervention strategy, her shift to a specialised area, or whatever else you have talked over, and are in danger of letting slide unless you build in the steps to encouragement and success.

An aspect of behavioural counselling that I respect is the mutual goal-setting, the close and realistic monitoring, and the emphasis that if the client falls down on achieving her goal, the counsellor has some responsibility in that. She was part of the goal-setting, and may have condoned unrealistic ambition. In just the same way, the supervisor's task in a review is perhaps to temper the ambitions of the counsellor to what is attainable in terms of time and that counsellor's character.

In a specially vivid way the review points up the supervisor's central task. She is there to encourage and assist the supervisee to become the best counsellor she can possibly be. That best will in part be to do with psychological theory, and with the detailed examination of how and what she communicates to her client.

The best is also to do with living in a way that leaves the counsellor free to love. The review is a chance to look at whether supervision, which mostly means you as supervisor, is taking the supervisee forward at the right pace towards self-confidence based on reality, towards valuing of herself and others, towards, in short, what Maslow called Abundance Motivation.

94

OTHER FLEAS

Great fleas have little fleas
Upon their backs to bite 'em.
Little fleas have lesser fleas,
And so ad infinitum.

How is the supervisor to be supervised? Or is she to sail along in the warm breezes of nothing more than her own sense of her worth? What else is she to do?

One crazy solution is hinted at in this chapter, in the tale of Mrs Cribbins and The Carpenter. In this, Mrs Cribbins was remote-control counselled by a series, a hierarchy of people. This was not supervision at all, to my mind. Nevertheless, supervisors need varying amounts of time, according to their work-load and experience, to look at how they are supervising, and, every so often, to glance along the line and talk a little about one of their supervisee's clients, about whom they feel they may not be responding well enough.

In training establishments, they are probably in contact with other staff, at least for the task of deciding whether a student is finally to be qualified and let loose on the public. In doing no more than this, taking care of the supervisor herself may be overlooked.

I see the need for her, the supervisor herself, to have an annual review, and regular staff meetings in which she can get a clearer view of the whole organisation in relation to herself. Such meetings need too to do some emotional maintenance work for everyone present, giving them a chance to do what my mother would call letting their hair down. They are an opportunity to cry or laugh together, and be less grown-up than at other times of their working life.

The aims of counselling are connected with psychic health. I feel suspicious of arrangements which leave the client carrying everyone's hopes of the possibility of living a rewarding life, while all the professionals run around obsessing, harassed or scrapping covertly among themselves, as sometimes happens. I think there is a good deal to be gained from looking at the setting of counselling as having some analogies with the rest of life, of which it is after all a part.

Part of the work is to plan for good experience, for occasional celebration where there is cause, and for meetings which fulfil their stated task, and also leave people feeling enhanced rather than diminished.

THE REFERENCE GROUP

The same constraints that are there for client and for counsellor exist for the supervisor and her institution or informal association. Time, distance and money are probably difficult. There will be hostile figures in the outer world as well as within. Added to that, most supervisors are qualified and experienced enough to know their job well. For most of their career they are unlikely to need close discussion of the content of it. But they need what some theorists call a reference group, which is a peer or colleague group where they have a sense of membership and support, and through which, formally or informally, they monitor themselves and have some exchange about their experience.

All that I am saying here applies as well to counsellors who from choice or necessity function without regular supervision. If they are experienced, they are probably, like supervisors, doing good work. But they need some monitoring, some fresh input, some association with people doing similar work, as well. In saying this, I would like to make clear that I am not at all in favour of supervision as a whole way of life. Like all luxuries, it will keep its value best, if it is not indulged in too much.

In one agency some years ago I came across the tale of Mrs Cribbins and her Carpenter. Mrs Cribbins turned up at a charitable social work agency of a specialist kind. She was a very dithery lady, apparently hell-bent on creating debt, chaos and discomfort around her. The agency was funded to deal with people with a certain disability, one with which she was somewhat tenuously connected. But the agency was worryingly short of clients. They took on Mrs Cribbins, who stated as her problem that she needed a carpenter, as two in succession had left her kitchen unusable, to the point of having no floorboards. After a case conference about her, her counsellor attempted to lead Mrs Cribbins into listening to herself, examining and evaluating her emotionality and her way of life, with a view to changing her behaviour in many notable respects.

Mrs Cribbins kept on about the carpenter.

In a dizzy moment the counsellor gave her the name of a good joiner. The next week Mrs Cribbins had turned her attention to electricians.

At this point the counsellor's supervisor pointed out the counsellor's foolishness in dealing at symptom level in this way. The counsellor wrung her hands, and they planned a more thorough strategy, for making Mrs Cribbins consider a whole new style of life.

The supervisor then talked to her principal about what she had done. As they had no other clients at all, the principal and regional director had a long shrewd evaluation of Mrs Cribbins, and what her counsellor should be doing. They had a meeting with the supervisor to pass on their valuable thoughts. When an outside consultant, me, arrived, I heard a tiny amount about the organisation, and a great deal about Mrs Cribbins.

All the people I met wanted to justify their existence, or at least their salaries, by worrying about Mrs Cribbins, rather than doing the looking inwards and starting a fresh new life that they were so keen to impose on her. Some publicity subsequently brought them a proper number of clients, and soon there was enough useful work around to keep people occupied. Mrs Cribbins found an electrician and left them.

For me there are many morals in this anecdote. One of them is about bad supervising. If the counsellor got flummoxed, then at least the supervisor should have had the wit to point out to her that she must explain to Mrs Cribbins that they were running a counselling service, not a kind of domestic Yellow Pages. Mrs Cribbins had not understood that, and why should she? If I walked in at a restaurant door, mistaking it for a hairdresser's, I should be bemused and annoyed to be sat down, handed a menu and told that eating is good for me. Of course it is. But not for me at that moment.

The central point that interested me here is the risk of over-supervision, in places where for one reason or other there is a make-work ethos. All the meetings I reported above, and there were a good number of each kind before I heard what was going on, took Mrs Cribbins as the focus.

Now to my mind it was the counsellor's job to deal with Mrs Cribbins. It was the supervisor's job to help the counsellor evaluate and possibly change how she was doing that. It was the principal's job to know if the supervisor had anything they needed to talk over. There might have been a decision to make about whether the counsellor needed to be sacked or given further training, for example. It was the director's job to see if funds were being spent in a proper manner and to best effect. But as so often in such organisations, everyone there had experience of work with clients and enjoyed this craft skill rather more than the administrative duties of their new posts. So confidentiality and good sense went out of the window, and an informal competition in hearsay psychoanalysis seemed to set in.

At least here there was some available support for the supervisor. Many others function out in the wilderness, with only occasional meetings within the professional body to which they respond. Time and again, the outside supervisor is a busy and somewhat prestigious figure, who squashes a few supervision sessions into another career. For her, as for experienced counsellors who do not have regular supervision, I suggest some occasional meetings.

THE BIENNALE

I advocate at least a biennial, if not an annual, seminar for all supervisors, specially those who are not otherwise taken care of in that role. The point of it I hope I have partly made clear already. As well, there is a good deal to be gained from letting them find out just how differently they all view the task, and do it.

How the event is set up will I hope be conditioned by who is going to attend. If all those there will be from the same discipline, there might be value in inviting someone from a different one to demonstrate some new approach to supervision, for part of the time. There may be interest in the presentation of one or two short papers.

A major feature of the day, however, is putting people into a usefully unfamiliar role. Instead of being the respected expert, they are back to being the kids in school. If the seminar is no more than the presentation of papers and the asking of clever questions about them, that shift of role may not be felt. There are plenty of academics and others who are used to conferences where they can play Shoot-Down-The-Speaker, by standing up in the body of the hall to make their own statements, which have little to do with anything except their own search for recognition. In this format they may not be having a fresh, or even a very enjoyable, experience.

I prefer that any paper is seen as a launch of small-group discussion, which does not necessarily have to end in wretched little reports back to the whole group. Where these are prescribed and required, rather than optional, some trite or far-fetched remarks can result. Again, if there are to be mostly formal, to-the-whole-group presentations, then I see the need for formal structuring of association.

At a large Old-Students rally of a counselling course run by South-West London College, a street map of London, and a large map of the whole country, were on the wall. Everyone attending had a number put by their name on a list at the entrance. This number was written on to a pin-label, which the relevant person was then invited to stick into the map near her address. Immediately you could see that number 49 lived in the next street or the same town as you, and could go and find his name on the list, and make contact with him via the name label everyone also wore. This exercise required a little forethought and equipment, but was not at all laborious to execute. It was a structure which seemed to deal excellently with my, and I think other people's, nervousness at arriving in a room mostly full of strangers.

If the numbers are suitable, the seminar can take the form of a supervision group, and so provide a model of how to set up a new one, and deal with the rivalrous feelings and insecurity as well as the more cheerful feelings and hopes in any such gathering.

One result of whatever form of meeting you think of, might be a useful experience-sharing and training day. Another would probably be the extending or strengthening of a local network of supervisors - the reference group. The discovery of new colleagues, even friends with the same work preoccupations, is well worth a few hours every year or two years.

THE WRITER

Gaie Houston, M.A., Oxon., Dip. A.B.Sc., has worked as a therapist, group and organisation consultant since she trained in the States in the late sixties. She was a lecturer on the S.W.London Counselling Course for seven years, and helped make that course student-centred. She has presented three television series on human behaviour, and writes plays for theatre and radio. As well as many one-to-one trainees and postgraduates, she supervises a number of staff groups, including those of training organisations, counselling agencies, and drug rehabilitation projects.

She is now a visiting lecturer at Universities and other institutions in the U.K. and other countries, consultant to the Gestalt Centre in London, and Director of the Rochester Foundation. This Foundation is a small group of experienced practitioners, who set up supervisory, educational, training and consultancy interventions in response to and co-operation with their clients.

All titles in the paperback Red Book Series written by Gaie Houston are available from book shops, or direct from :- The Rochester Foundation, 8, Rochester Terrace, London NW1 9JN. Cheques for £4.95 a copy should be made out to Gaie Houston and sent with orders to the above address. The titles so far are:

SUPERVISION AND COUNSELLING ISBN 0 9510323 2 1

THE RED BOOK OF GESTALT   ISBN 0 9510323 4 8

THE RED BOOK OF GROUPS, [AND HOW TO LEAD THEM BETTER]   ISBN 0 9510323 3 X